An
American
Sunrise

当代国际诗人典译丛书

美洲的黎明

Joy Harjo

[美] 风欢乐◎著

迟 欣◎译

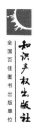

知识产权出版社

全国百佳图书出版单位

图书在版编目(CIP)数据

美洲的黎明:汉英对照/[美]风欢乐著;迟欣译.—北京:知识产权出版社,
2016.6

(当代国际诗人典译丛书)

ISBN 978-7-5130-3860-7

Ⅰ.①美… Ⅱ.①风… ②迟… Ⅲ.①英语—汉语—对照读物
②诗集—美国—现代 Ⅳ.①H319.4:I

中国版本图书馆 CIP 数据核字(2015)第 247157 号

内容提要

本双语版诗集是"当代国际诗人典译丛书"(一套五册)其中的一本,由美国印第安女诗人风欢乐(Joy Harjo)精心甄选的三十三首诗歌组成,除一首新诗外,其他分别选自她七部不同的诗集。其诗歌继承了印第安人的口述传统,用记忆的细线串联起了印第安人历史上的重要瞬间;诗歌中的坚强意志和山河壮美是诗人对抗印第安精神创伤的智慧。诗人将对自由的追寻化作诗句,凭借勇气不断搜寻民族文化中精彩的记忆故事;以纯然、朴实之心沉浸于印第安人的生活,穿越人性被残害和扭曲的时代,透露出对人生的独特感悟。这一切使得她的诗歌散发出热烈、淳朴、激昂、自然的芬芳。

责任编辑:陈晶晶 **责任出版:孙婷婷**

美洲的黎明

[美]风欢乐 著 迟欣 译

出版发行:知识产权出版社 有限责任公司		网 址:http://www.ipph.cn	
社 址:北京市海淀区西外太平庄 55 号		邮 编:100081	
责编电话:010-82000860 转 8391		责编邮箱:shiny-chjj@163.com	
发行电话:010-82000860 转 8101/8102		发行传真:010-82000893/82005070/82000270	
印 刷:北京中献拓方科技发展有限公司		经 销:各大网上书店、新华书店及相关专业书店	
开 本:720mm×960mm 1/32		印 张:5.75	
版 次:2016 年 6 月第 1 版		印 次:2016 年 6 月第 1 次印刷	
字 数:120 千字		定 价:25.00 元	

ISBN 978-7-5130-3860-7

译者序

　　2014年8月通过北京的挚友，幸运地与知识产权出版社的美女编辑陈晶晶相识。获悉晶晶正在着手出版《当代国际诗人典译丛书》。这卷丛书汇集了五位当代活跃于世界诗坛的顶尖诗人的精选作品，均为首次于国内出版，并完全由知识产权出版社资助完成。面对如此优秀的诗歌选集，我斗胆承接了美国印第安女性诗人风欢乐（Joy Harjo）诗歌作品的翻译任务。当然，由此也着实给我带来了不小的压力。我是学文学出身，对美国诗歌也算情有独钟。也曾以美国"垮掉派"诗人为主题出版过学术专著，在专著当中，为了研究的需要，我也翻译了近百首诗歌。尽管如此，出版诗歌译本，却是人生的第一次。因此，翻译的文笔和对原文的把握，或许显得有些青涩而稚嫩，唯有希望这个译本能够基本表达出诗人的思想和情感。

　　风欢乐（1951—　）是美国一位多才多艺的印第安女性诗人，她不仅从事诗歌创作，同时还担任"诗歌正义（Poetic Justice）"乐队中的萨克斯管乐手，并在多部文学评论期刊担任编辑。另外，风欢乐还经常利用乐队演出间歇，撰写电影和电视剧本、公益广告以及电视教育节目。本次出版的双语诗集包括诗人亲自甄选的三十三首诗歌，除却一首新诗外，分别选自她7部不同的诗集。为了纪念她的诗选能够在中国出版，风欢乐坚持诗选的封面使用自己起的中文姓名：疯欢乐。

"欢乐"当然是英文"Joy"的本意，而"Harjo"则是印第安语中"疯狂"（crazy）的意思。但是把"疯"使用在名字当中，似乎有伤大雅，也有点难以被中国读者接受。后来在中国学者的建议之下，她同意使用"风欢乐"作为自己的中文姓名——一个充满自由意味的名字。小小名字的抉择却折射出诗人对中国文化的尊重，以及对其本人印第安血统的骄傲与自豪。

风欢乐的诗歌记述了印第安人被"殖民"后的苦难历史，具备积极振奋的责任意识和伦理精神的她对这份苦难进行了顽强抗争。其诗歌中的坚强诗意和山河壮美是风欢乐对抗印第安精神创伤的智慧。诗人凭借勇气与智慧不断搜寻民族文化中精彩的记忆故事，她进入历史，将历史再现，并不断超越严峻的现实。

风欢乐的诗歌从节奏、措辞和表达方式上尽可能地体现印第安民族口述历史的传统。比如，在诗集的最后一首近乎散文的诗歌"为圣人消解冲突（*From Conflict*

Resolution for Holy Beings）"里面，风欢乐将那段印第安的苦难历史如同讲故事般娓娓道来，恰如行云流水，初无定质，常行于所当行，止于不可不止。因此，她诗歌的韵律几乎是自由诗的形式，追求的节奏不是人为事先规定，而是自然天成。

　　鉴于其诗歌风格，我在翻译的过程中，比较关注源文本和目的语文本的语言表达、内容阐释等方面，基本采取了忠实于原文的直译方法。尽可能地完整体现原文的意图和文本的实现过程，保持原文内容的和谐与固有的形式。另外，对部分中国读者不太熟悉的文化、地理、历史等方面的知识点做了注释。个别的风景诗歌，因为考虑到目的语文化的差异、中国读者接受的效果、义化选择等社会文化方面的关系，我采用了意译的形式，力图通过诗歌韵律来展现令诗人缱绻眷念的美洲大地的秀丽风光。

　　最后需要说明的是，风欢乐本人坚持选定"美洲的黎明（*An American Sunrise*）"作为本诗集的书名。同时，这也是她的新诗"美洲的黎明"的名字。该诗创作的灵感源于美国黑人女诗人高文德琳·布鲁克斯（Gwendolyn Brooks，1917—2000）的一首短诗"我们真酷（*We Real Cool*）"。风欢乐曾坦言布鲁克斯对她的影响很大。这首诗歌，很明显地模仿了布鲁克斯"金铲式诗歌"（Golden Shovel poem）的风格。为了让读者更好地理解风欢乐的诗歌，我把布鲁克斯的诗歌也翻译如下。

We Real Cool

The Pool Players
Seven at the Golden Shovel.

We real cool. We
Left school. We

Lurk late. We
Strike straight. We

Sing sin. We
Thin gin. We

Jazz June. We
Die soon.

我们真酷

弹子球的游戏者
有七个，在"金铲"游戏厅。

我们真酷。我们
离校逃课。我们

深夜潜行。我们
大打出手。我们

高歌罪恶。我们
开怀畅饮。我们

六月歌舞。我们
一命呜呼。

布鲁克斯在这首短诗里以调侃的口吻描绘了二十世纪六十年代的年轻人懒散放纵、酒醉嬉闹的生活方式与态度。风欢乐则在诗"美洲的黎明"中呼吁印第安的年轻人决不能有这样行尸走肉般的游戏人生。印第安人应该有自己的思想、自己的宗教、自己的奋斗目标和自己的未来。风欢乐如布鲁克斯一样，把每个诗节的第二行的第一个词"We"移至前一行的末尾，使部分诗歌成为跨行诗。同时，每个诗节的第二行和第三行的最后一个词全部押头韵或尾韵，并且借用了布鲁克斯诗歌的原词。通过这样的技巧，风欢乐极力渲染和强调该诗乃至整部译诗集的主题：她一次次地拒绝着主流文化的同化，一次次地倾吐出对独特的印第安传统部族文化的认同、关注与热爱。

薰风微雨的初夏，风欢乐的诗歌选集《美洲的黎明》马上就要出版了。就在二零一五年的九月，风欢乐获得了"华莱士·史蒂文斯大奖（Wallace Stevens Award）"，这是美国诗歌创作界极具影响力的奖项之一。这个奖项的获得是对风欢乐多年为印第安人权利奔走、呼吁的肯定，同时，似乎也是对中国这部双语选集出版的庆祝。作为我的处女译本，该诗集必定会有很多不尽如人意的地方，恳请各位同行、专家、学者以及读者批评、斧正。在翻译过程中，衷心感谢天津科技大学的王振平教授和中国民航大学的鄢佳老师对该诗歌译本的倾情帮助；也再次感谢陈晶晶编辑对该书耐心、细致的校正工作。

迟　欣
2016年初夏

致读者

亲爱的喜爱这些诗歌和希冀飞翔的读者：

我笃信，诗歌尽管有着不同的支派，但它们却来源于同一个根系。站在邻近的星球边缘去观察地球，地球何其小！北美的这片部落领土是我从事写作的地方，如果我们是以歌声而非英里（抑或是千米）来丈量，中国与之并不遥远。诗歌发轫于大众对歌唱的集体诉求。间或，先祖的歌声会穿透我们的心灵。他们可能是人类的先祖，也可能是石头、风、动物或者其他元素的先祖。我着实不可能被冠以诗人的称谓。我的邻里们也不会有人将自己唤作"诗人"，尽管过去或现在的歌曲总是蕴含着诗意。以我们部族传统的眼光来看，诗歌之所以存在，是因为音乐和舞蹈的存在。诗歌如果没有了音乐和舞蹈这样的伙伴，只能变得越来越孤独。而我，没有诗歌的陪伴，也只能是越来越落寞。当我还是个年轻的母亲，当我还在大学学习艺术学的时候，诗之精灵就闯入了我的心怀。这的确不是一条容易走的道路，我几度想

and I often wanted to give up. The spirit of poetry came to me and said, "You are coming with me! You do not know how to listen. You need to learn grace. I will show you." I listened. I am still listening to the songs that rise up into words.

May you find something in these speaking songs to inspire you, to open your heart's ears.

Respectfully,

Joy Harjo

要放弃。但是诗之精灵向我走来，对我说："跟我一起来吧！你还不知道如何聆听。你需要学会什么是优雅。来，我教你！"我听从了她的安排。于是，我将不断地聆听渗透进语言里的歌声。

亲爱的读者，你或许会发现隐藏在这些动听歌曲背后的某些东西，它们将激励着你的人生，打开你的心扉。

此致
敬礼！

风欢乐

目录
Contents

目录
Contents

From *How We Became Human,*
New and Selected Poems
1975—2001

Equinox

I must keep from breaking into the story by force,
If I do I will find a war club in my hand
And the smoke of grief staggering toward the sun,
Your nation dead beside you.

I keep walking away though it has been an eternity
And from each drop of blood
Springs up sons and daughters, trees
A mountain of sorrows, of songs.

I tell you this from the dusk of a small city in the north
Not far from the birthplace of cars and industry.
Geese are returning to mate and crocuses have
Broken through the frozen earth.

Soon they will come for me and I will make my stand
Before the jury of destiny. Yes, I will answer in the clatter
Of the new world, I have broken my addiction to war
And desire. Yes, I will reply, I have buried the dead

And made songs of the blood, the marrow.

春 分

我克制自己通过武力成为故事的主角，
假若真要如此，我岂不要手舞军棍
痛苦如烟，袅袅飘向太阳，
你的国家消亡，就在你身旁。

我选择离开，尽管它已不朽
一滴滴鲜血
孕育了儿女、树木
还有说不完的痛苦，唱不尽的歌谣。

黄昏，我把一切告诉你，在北方小城
与汽车和工业的发源地毗邻。
大雁飞回北方寻觅伴侣，藏红花
冲破冻土，焕发生机。

不久大雁就会向我飞来，我亦将
伫立在掌管命运的陪审团前。是的，我会在
喧嚣的新大陆上应答，我已斩断自己与战争和欲望
的联系。是的，我应答，我已将死者埋葬。

谱写一曲流血之歌，是精髓。

No

Yes that was me you saw shaking with bravery, with a
government issued rifle on my back. I'm sorry I could not
greet you, as you deserved, my relative.

They were not my tears. I have a reservoir inside. They will
be cried by my sons, my daughters if I can't learn how to
turn tears to stone.

Yes, that was me standing in the back door of the house in
the alley, with fresh corn and bread for the neighbors.

I did not foresee the flood of blood. How they would forget our
friendship, would return to kill the babies and me.

Yes, that was me whirling on the dance floor. We made
such a racket with all that joy. I loved the whole world in
that silly music.

I did not realize the terrible dance in the staccato of bullets.

不

是的，这就是你眼中的我，因为勇敢而舞动腰肢，背上
扛着政府准许携带的枪支。亲人啊，我无法带给你所预
期的祝福，愧疚难当。

它们不是我的泪水。我的泪水深埋于心底。倘若无法做到
铁石心肠，我的子女将为之哭泣。

是的，的确是我站在小巷深处，房屋的后门边，为邻里
带来新鲜的谷物和面包。

我没能预见血流成河。他们怎能忘却我们的友谊，转身
就残害了我的孩子，还有我。

是的，我在地板上旋转飞舞。我们
因为欢乐而纵情喧闹。在令人眩晕的乐曲声中，
我挚爱这个世界。

我没有意识到那枪林弹雨中可怕的舞步。

Yes. I smelled the burning grease of corpses. And like a fool I expected our words might rise up and jam the artillery in the hands of dictators.

We had to keep going. We sang our grief to clean the air of turbulent spirits.

Yes, I did see the terrible black clouds as I cooked dinner. And the messages of the dying spelled there in the ashy sunset. Every one addressed: "mother".

There was nothing about it in the news. Everything was the same. Unemployment was up. Another queen crowned with flowers. Then there were the sports scores.

Yes, the distance was great between your country and mine. Yet our children played in the path between our houses.

No. We had no quarrel with each other.

是的。我闻到了尸油的气味。我就像个傻瓜，
竟然渴望我的言语能被人关注，并能阻断独裁者的狂轰滥炸。

我们必须永不止步。我们歌唱，痛苦地歌唱，以安抚
动荡、紊乱的情绪。

是的，备餐之刻，我看到了可怕的乌云。
死亡的咒语从日暮后灰色的天际
隐约传来。所有的人都在呼唤："母亲。"

新闻对此只字未提。
依旧。失业率飙升。新皇后戴着花冠
加冕。还有体育赛场上的欢腾。

是的，你我的住地相距遥远。
然我们的孩子在你我家园间的小道上玩耍。

不。我们之间没有龃龉。

Evening Song or No Huli

We failed a little

Dip the wound in water

Wrap it in a song

Climb in the canoe

And paddle out from the weeping

Let the failing fail

Let the stars bear trouble

Let the canoe carry

What we cannot bury.

暮歌，永不言败[①]

一场小小的失败

宛若在水中浸过的伤口

以歌声包扎

登上一叶扁舟

长声呜咽，扁舟驶离

让失败灰飞烟灭吧

让繁星承载哀愁

让扁舟带走

我们无法埋葬的一切。

---

① 作者曾在夏威夷生活了十二年。Huli系夏威夷语。意思是"翻转""翻船"。No Huli的意思是"不会翻船"，译者将其意译为"永不言败"。

It's Raining in Honolulu

There is a small mist at the brow of the mountain,
Each leaf of flower, of taro, tree and bush shivers with ecstasy.

And the rain songs of all the flowering ones who have called for the rain
Can be found there, flourishing beneath the currents of singing.

Rain opens us, like flowers, or earth that has been thirsty for
more than a season.

We stop all of our talking, quit thinking, to drink the mystery.
We listen to the breathing beneath our breathing.
We hear how the rain became rain, how we became human.

The wetness saturates and cleans everything, including the perpetrators
Of the second overthrow.

We will plant songs where there were curses.

檀香山的雨

薄雾笼罩山脊,
鲜花的叶子、香芋的叶子,还有绿树和灌木从欢乐得发狂。

所有祈雨的花儿欢唱着雨的颂歌,
嘹亮的歌声绚烂了花朵。

雨水敞开了我们的心扉,宛若花儿绽放
大地已经期盼甘霖多时,如饥似渴。

我们终止了所有的闲谈,放弃了所有的思考,去品味每一分神秘。
我们聆听从心底传出的呼声。
我们倾听雨水如何化作雨水,我们又如何成为人类。

湿漉漉的空气浸润了一切,荡涤了一切,哪怕是屡次违法的罪犯
也因此心灵圣洁。

我们在充满咒语的地方埋下歌声的种子。

Watching Crow, Looking South
Towards the Manzano Mountains

crow floats in winter sun

a black sliver

in a white ocean of sky

crow is the horizon

drifting south of Albuquerque

the horizon dances

along the blue edge

of the Manzanos

wind is an arch

a curve

on the black wing of crow

a warm south wind

if it stays for awhile

will keep a crow dancing for thirty years

on the ridge

of a blue mountain breeze

观鸦，南望曼扎诺山脉①

冬日暖阳，寒鸦飞翔
天海一色，黛青飞影
阿尔布开克②以南，
寒鸦展翅
隐于天涯

地平线与曼扎诺的
青青山脊
共舞
风儿潇潇，
似一道圆弧，
与黑鸦一点，两茫茫。

温暖的南风
拂面
驻足少顷
寒鸦会翩翩起舞三十载
在青青山脊。

① 曼扎诺山脉（Manzano Mountains）位于美国新墨西哥州中部，南北走向，绵延大约六十五千米。
② 阿尔布开克（Albuquerque）为美国新墨西哥州的中部城市。

From *In Mad Love and War*

Eagle Song

To pray, you open your whole self

To sky, to earth, to sun, to moon

To one whole voice that is you.

And know that there is more

That you can't see, can't hear

Can't know, except in moments

Steadily growing

and in languages that aren't always sound

But other circles of motion

Like eagle that Sunday morning

Over Salt River

Circled in blue sky, in wind

Swept our hearts clean with sacred wings

We see you see ourselves

And know that we must take

The utmost care and kindness

In all things

Breathe in knowing we are made of all of this

And breathe, knowing we are truly blessed because we were

born and die soon within a true circle of motion.

鹰之歌

祈祷，你展开翅膀
奔向蓝天、土地、太阳和月亮
放声歌唱。
你知晓，有很多事物
你无法看到、无法听见
也无法明了，除非在能够
顽强生长的那一刻
除非能以不常言说的话语
然而，其他的循环往复
如同星期天早晨的鹰
　飞过盐河
盘旋于碧空，在风中
拍着圣洁的翅膀，荡涤我们的心房
我们明白你早已看穿了我们
深知我们要以
极大的关怀与仁慈
对待万事万物
明晰我们是如此组成
并生存于世，亦知我们的确幸运，来也匆匆，去也匆匆
那才是真实的人生循环

Like eagle, rounding out the morning inside us

We pray that it will be done

In beauty, in beauty

如那只苍鹰，令我们心中清晨的模样趋于完美
我们祈祷这愿望将在
美好与美妙中达成

Rainy Dawn

I can still close my eyes and open them four floors up looking south and west from the hospital, the approximate direction of Acoma, and farther on to the roofs of the houses of the gods who have learned there are no endings, only beginnings. That day so hot, heat danced in waves off bright car tops, we both stood poised at that door from the east, listened for a long time to the sound of our grandmothers' voices, the brushing wind of sacred wings, the rattle of raindrops in dry gourds. I had to participate in the dreaming of you into mem—cupped your head in the bowl of my body as ancestors lined up to give you a name made of their dreams cast once more into this stew of precious spirit and flesh. And let you go, as I am letting you go once more in this ceremony of the living. And when you were born I held you wet and unfolding, like a butterfly newly born from the chrysalis of my body. And breathed with you as you breathed your first breath. Then was your promise to take it on like the rest of us, this immense journey, for love, for rain.

雨中黎明[①]

我依然还能闭上双眼，再次睁开的时候，站在四层楼高的医院向西和南远眺，医院大约在埃克马[②]的方向，父亲正在攀上神灵的房屋之顶，他们深谙事情远未结束，一切才刚刚开始。那一天酷热难耐，热浪翻滚，向汽车顶棚袭来，我们父女二人在朝东向的大门口驻足，聆听祖母的歌声良久，歌声似神圣的羽翼带来的微风，似雨滴敲打在干瘪葫芦上的噼噼啪啪的响声。我产生了拥有你的梦想，将你的小脑袋放进我的身体，此刻，祖辈们争相踊跃地为你起一个承载着世代梦想的名字，而这个梦想又不断地在宝贵的精神和肉体中孕育生长。放开你的手，我再一次在这个人生的舞台放开你的手，让你走。当你呱呱坠地，我拥着湿漉漉的、没有被襁褓围裹的你，像一只从我的身体里破茧而出的蝴蝶。当你第一次呼吸，我的命运就与你紧紧地连在了一起。随后，如同我们所有的人，有关你的预言将逐一呈现，这是人生的漫漫长途，因为爱，因为雨。

---

① 这首诗是诗人在女儿十三岁生日时为其所作。阿尔布开克（Albuquerque）的雨水稀少，因而异常珍贵。而作者小女儿出生在一个炎热的7月，刚好下了一场大雨，作者由此为女儿取名Rain Dawn。

② 埃克马（Acoma）是美国新墨西哥州颇具特色的一个印第安村落，由于建在高地上而被称为"空中之城(Sky City)"。——译者注

Grace

I think of Wind and her wild ways the year we had nothing to lose
and lost it anyway in the cursed country of the fox. We still
talk about that winter, how the cold froze imaginary buffalo on
the stuffed horizon of snow banks. The haunting voices of the starved
and mutilated broke fences, crashed our thermostat dreams, and we couldn't
stand it one more time. So once again we lost a winter in stubborn
memory, walked through cheap apartment walls, skated through fields of
ghosts into a town that never wanted us, in the epic search for grace.

Like Coyote, like Rabbit, we could not contain our terror and
clowned our way through a season of false midnights. We had to
swallow that town with laughter, so it would go down easy as honey.
And one morning as the sun struggled to break ice, and our dreams had
found us with coffee and pancakes in a truck stop along Highway 80,
we found grace.

I could say grace was a woman with time on her hands, or a white
buffalo escaped from memory. But in that dingy light it was a
promise of balance. We once again understood the talk of animals, and
spring was lean and hungry with the hope of children and corn.

恩 泽

我思念风儿和它狂野的个性，还有我们一无所有的时光
我们在狐狸般狡猾的国度里，丧失了所有。我们仍旧谈
论着那个冬日，谈论着寒冷如何将幻想中的野牛冰冻在路边
坚实的雪丘之上。饥肠辘辘、羸弱枯瘦的人们，号叫声
冲破藩篱，撞击着我们温暖的梦境，我们不堪
忍受。于是，我们在已经凝固的记忆中，失却了冬天，
穿过廉价的公寓房，滑过幽灵出没的田野，躲进
连魔鬼都不屑光顾的小镇，漫长而艰难地寻觅着恩泽。

如郊狼，似野兔，我们无法掩饰恐惧，
笨手笨脚地一路穿过虚幻的午夜。我们不得不
狂笑着吞掉这个城镇，就像吞咽流淌的蜂蜜。
清晨，当太阳挣扎着融化坚冰，我们的梦想察觉到
我们在80号公路边的火车站品着咖啡，尝着薄饼，
沐浴着恩泽。

我说，恩泽是一个手托时间的女人，抑或是
逃出记忆的白色野牛。然而在暗淡的灯光下，它是信守的
诺言。我们再次理解了动物间的交谈和
春季的萧条与青黄不接，渴望孩子们成长，庄稼发芽。

I would like to say, with grace, we picked ourselves up and
walked into the spring thaw. We didn't; the next season was worse.
You went home to Leech Lake to work with the tribe and I went south.
And, Wind, I am still crazy. I know there is something larger than the
memory of a dispossessed people. We have seen it.

我想说，我们沐浴恩泽，出发，

走进春天，冰消雪化。我们原地不动，未来的时日就会更糟。

你回到水蛭湖畔①的家乡，与那里的部族共事，而我已奔赴南方。

风儿啊，我依然狂野。我明了，有些超越了记忆的东西

记忆中人类丧失了家园。我们作证。

---

① 水蛭湖（Leech Lake）位于美国明尼苏达州中北部，那里是美国印第安人保护区。

Bird

The moon plays horn, leaning on the shoulder of the dark universe
to the infinite glitter of chance. Tonight I watched Bird kill himself,

larger than real life. I've always had a theory that some of us
are born with nerve endings longer than our bodies. Out to here,

farther than his convoluted scales could reach. Those nights he
played did he climb the stairway of forgetfulness, with his horn,

a woman who is always beautiful to strangers? All poets
understand the final uselessness of words. We are chords to

other chords to other chords, if we're lucky, to melody. The moon
is brighter than anything I can see when I come out of the theater,

than music, than memory of music, or any mere poem. At least

鸟

斜倚在幽暗宇宙的肩头，月神①吹起了号角
为了无尽的命运之旅。今夜，我目睹了鸟儿的自戕，

如同一个传奇。我总以为，有些人
生来神经末梢要长过身体。甚至

长过月神那精密复杂的刻尺度。那些夜晚，他
用他的号角弹唱，逾越了忘却的天梯。

陌生人面前，女人是不是总会优雅美丽？所有的诗人
都明白语言最终会变得苍白无力。我们和着，

和着，不断地和着，如果幸运，就会合上节拍。月光
分外明亮，当我走出剧场，

连乐曲、对乐曲的记忆，还有诗歌，都无法与这月光媲美。至少，

---

　　① 在印第安神话中，日神和月神由一对兄弟所变。传说，兄弟二人
射杀了太阳和月亮之后，哥哥当了太阳，弟弟娶了月亮的女儿，"从此，
月亮弟弟跟着太阳哥哥日夜不停地环游太空"。因此，该诗中的月神为男
性，并非意指希腊、罗马等神话中的女性月神。——译者注

I can dance to "Ornithology" or sweet–talk beside "Charlie's Blues",

but inside this poem I can't play a horn, hijack a plane to
somewhere where music is the place those nerve endings dangle.

Each rhapsody embodies counterpoint, and pain stuns the woman
in high heels, the man behind the horn, sings the heart.

To survive is sometimes a leap into madness. The fingers of
saints are still hot from miracles, but can they save themselves?

Where is the dimension a god lives who will take Bird home?
I want to see it, I said to the Catalinas, to the Rincons,

to anyone listening in the dark. I said, Let me hear you
by any means: by horn, by fever, by night, even by some poem

attempting flight home.

我可以和着《鸟》①的乐曲曼舞，或和着《查理的蓝调》②甜美吟唱。

然而，在诗歌里，我无法吹响号角，无法劫持飞机前往
飘满音乐的地方，于此，我的每一个神经末梢会徘徊、陶醉。

每一首狂想曲都是复调的手法，高跟鞋
让女人倍感疼痛，男人却吹着号角，真情欢唱。

有的时候为了活着就得跳入疯狂的深渊。圣人的手指
依然火热，因为创造了奇迹，但是他们是否可以将自己拯救？

神祇们住在哪里才能将鸟儿带回家乡？
我想见到它，我对卡达琳纳③人说，对里肯人说，

对任何一个身处黑暗中聆听的人说。我说，让我聆听你内心的倾诉，
以任何方式：号角，狂热，夜晚，哪怕是几首诗歌

打算飞一般地回家。

---

① 《鸟（Ornithology）》是美国爵士乐钢琴家Al Haig（1922—
1982）的波普爵士音乐专辑。

② 《查理的蓝调（Charlie's Blues）》是美国布鲁斯（又称蓝调）
音乐家的作品，曾获格莱美音乐奖。

③ 卡达琳纳（Catalina）与下文提到的里肯（Rincon）是美国亚利
桑那州南部城市图森（Tucson）附近的山脉。

From *The Woman Who Fell
From the Sky*

Perhaps the Word Ends Here

The world begins at a kitchen table. No matter what, we
must eat to live.

The gifts of earth are brought and prepared, set on the table.
So it has been since creation, and it will go on.

We chase chickens or dogs away from it. Babies teethe at the corners.
They scrape their knees under it.

It is here that children are given instructions on what it means to be human.
We make men at it, we make women.

At this table we gossip, recall enemies and the ghosts of lovers.

Our dreams drink coffee with us as they put their arms
around our children. They laugh with us at our poor falling–down
selves and as we put ourselves back together once again at the table.

This table has been a house in the rain, an umbrella in the sun.

或许世界就此终结

世界始于厨房里的餐桌。沧海桑田，为了活着，我们
总得吃饭。

大地为我们准备了厚礼，呈于桌上。
从创世之初，延续至今日，并且依然会持续。

我们将小鸡和小狗儿从桌旁赶走。桌角边是孩子们咬过的齿印。
餐桌下，他们擦伤了膝盖。

桌边，孩子们接受着人类生存意义的教育。
桌边，我们创造了男人，我们创造了女人。

桌边，我们闲言碎语，追忆着对手，还有恋人的幽魂。

梦想和我们一起呷着咖啡，并将手臂挽着孩子们的
肩头。梦想与我们一起嘲笑着贫穷、落魄的自己
我们再一次将自己拽回到餐桌旁。

这只餐桌曾是雨中的房屋、阳光下的遮阳伞。

Wars have begun and ended at this table. It is a place to hide
in the shadow of terror. A place to celebrate the terrible victory.

We have given birth on this table, and have prepared our
parents for burial here.

At this table we sing with joy, with sorrow. We pray of
suffering and remorse. We give thanks.

Perhaps the world will end at the kitchen table, while we are
laughing and crying, eating of the last sweet bite.

战争从餐桌边伊始，亦在餐桌旁结束。餐桌是恐怖阴影
下的藏身之所。亦是庆贺来之不易的凯旋之地。

我们曾在餐桌边生儿育女，我们也曾在餐桌旁为父母准备
葬礼。

桌边，我们唱过欢歌，吟过悲曲。我们祈祷，为磨难
与懊悔。以此表达我们的谢意。

或许世界将终结于厨房里的餐桌，此刻，我们会
狂笑，会哭泣，吃一口最后的美餐。

Creation Story

I'm not afraid of love
or its consequence of light.

It's not easy to say this
or anything when my entrails
dangle between paradise
and fear.

I am ashamed
I never had the words
to carry a friend from her death
to the stars correctly.

Or the words to keep
my people safe
from drought or gunshot.

The stars who were created by words
are circling over this house
formed of calcium, of blood

创世的故事

我不会因为爱情
和它的虚无缥缈，而诚惶诚恐。

难以诉说
我的五脏六腑
在天堂与恐惧间摇摆
的微妙感受。

我羞愧万分
我从来不会用语言
从死神手里将朋友唤回
带她到应该去的星球。

也不会用语言让
我的人民从洪水或战争中
平安脱逃。

语言创造的繁星
盘旋于我们房屋的上空
这是座由钙和鲜血建成的房屋。

this house
in danger of being torn apart
by stones of fear.

If these words can do anything
if these songs can do anything
I say bless this house
with stars.

Transfix us with love.

顽固的恐惧感让

这个房屋

岌岌可危。

如果这些语言能做什么

如果这些乐曲能做什么

我会与繁星一起为这个房屋

祈福。

爱情让我们如痴如醉。

A Postcolonial Tale

Every day is a reenactment of the creation story. We emerge from
dense unspeakable material, through the shimmering power of
dreaming stuff.

This is the first world, and the last.

Once we abandoned ourselves for television, the box that
separates the dreamer from the dreaming. It was as if we were stolen,
put into a bag carried on the back of a Whiteman who pretends to
own the earth and the sky. In the sack were all the people of the
world. We fought until there was a hole in the bag.

When we fell we were not aware of falling. We were driving
to work, or to the mall. The children were in school learning
subtraction with guns.

We found ourselves somewhere near the diminishing point
of civilization, not far from the trickster's bag of tricks. Everything
was as we imagined it. The earth and stars, every creature
and leaf imagined with us.

后殖民时期的传说

每一天都是创世故事的重现。我们诞生于
厚重而又无法言喻的物质，穿过梦幻的微弱
光亮。

这是最初的世界，也是最终的世界。

一旦我们把自己交给了电视，这个方匣子就拉远了
追梦人与梦想之间的距离。如同我们被偷袭，被扔进
一个白人背着的大口袋里，他假称自己是
地球与天空的主宰。口袋里装着全世界的人。我们
奋勇抗争，终于把口袋捅破了一个洞。

我们从洞里"跌落"，却丝毫未觉。我们驱车去工作，
抑或去逛街。孩子们在学堂里学习加减乘除，
怀里揣着枪支。

我们已经徘徊在文明毁灭的边缘，与
无赖们装满骗局的口袋近在咫尺。一切
均在预料之中。地球和星星，每一种生物
和树叶与我们一起展开想象的翅膀。

When we fell we were not aware of falling. We were

driving to work or to the mall. The children were in school learning subtraction

with guns.

The imagining needs praise as does any living thing.

We are evidence of this praise.

And when we laugh, we're indestructible.

No story or song will translate

the full impact of falling,

or the inverse power of rising up.

Of rising up.

Our children put down their guns when we did to imagine with us.

We imagined the shining link between the heart and the sun.

We imagined tables of food for everyone.

We imagined the songs.

The imagination conversely illumines us, speaks with us,

sings with us, drums with us, loves us.

我们从洞里"跌落"，却丝毫未觉。我们驱车去工作，
抑或去逛街。孩子们在学堂里学习加减乘除，
怀里揣着枪支。

想象是需要赞扬的，任何生物都需要赞扬。
我们就是这种赞扬的证明。
我们狂笑，我们坚不可摧。
不会有故事，不会有歌曲将
这种衰落的影响，
抑或是阻碍上升的力量，诠释。
一股上升的力量。

我们的孩子放下了武器，与我们一道拍打着想象的翅膀。
我们想象着心灵与太阳之间熠熠闪光的纽带。
我们想象着为所有人预备好满桌的宴席。
我们想象着歌声飞扬。

反之，想象亦将我们点亮，与我们一起交流，
与我们一起歌唱，与我们一起击鼓，爱着我们。

From *She Had Some Horses*

She Had Some Horses

She had some horses.

She had horses who were bodies of sand.

She had horses who were maps drawn of blood.

She had horses who were skins of ocean water.

She had horses who were the blue air of sky.

She had horses who were fur and teeth.

She had horses who were clay and would break.

She had horses who were splintered red cliff.

She had some horses.

She had horses with eyes of trains.

She had horses with full, brown thighs.

She had horses who laughed too much.

She had horses who threw rocks at glass houses.

She had horses who licked razor blades.

She had some horses.

She had horses who danced in their mothers' arms.

She had horses who thought they were the sun and their

bodies shone and burned like stars.

她曾有几匹马

她曾有几匹马。
她的马，是一粒粒尘沙。
她的马，是血绘的地图。
她的马，是海面的波纹。
她的马，是碧蓝的天空。
她的马，是皮毛与牙齿。
她的马，是黏土，并具摧毁的力量。
她的马，是有裂缝的红色悬崖。
她曾有几匹马。

她的马，有经过训练的厉眼。
她的马，有健硕的棕色马腿。
她的马，欢欣雀跃。
她的马，向玻璃房子投掷石块。
她的马，舔舐着剃刀的锋刃。
她曾有几匹马。

她的马，在母亲的臂弯里起舞。
她的马，视自己为太阳，
马身熠熠闪光，似空中的繁星。

She had horses who waltzed nightly on the moon.

She had horses who were much too shy, and kept quiet
in stalls of their own making.

She had some horses.

She had horses who liked Creek Stomp Dance songs.

She had horses who cried in their beer.

She had horses who spit at male queens who made
them afraid of themselves.

She had horses who said they weren't afraid.

She had horses who lied.

She had horses who told the truth, who were stripped
bare of their tongues.

She had some horses.

She had horses who called themselves, "horse".

She had horses who called themselves, "spirit", and kept
their voices secret and to themselves.

She had horses who had no names.

She had horses who had books of names.

She had some horses.

她的马，夜夜在月宫跳华尔兹。

她的马，羞涩腼腆，娴雅宁静

圈于盛满草料的马厩。

她曾有几匹马。

她的马，钟爱克里克人①顿足爵士舞曲。

她的马，曾在饮酒时哭泣。

她的马，唾弃那些脂粉气太重的男性，

他们会让自己心生恐惧。

她的马，说他们无所畏惧。

她的马，会撒谎。

她的马，亦吐真言，却被剥夺了

话语的权利。

她曾有几匹马。

她的马，将自己唤作"骏马"。

她的马，将自己唤作"幽灵天使"，将

自己的声音隐匿，埋藏于心底。

她的马，是无名之辈。

她的马，名垂史册。

她曾有几匹马。

---

① 克里克人（Creek），是北美印第安人的一支，原居住在
佐治亚和亚拉巴马州的大片平地，经济以种植玉蜀黍、豆类及南
瓜为主。一般妇女耕作，男子外出狩猎或作战。

She had horses who whispered in the dark, who were afraid to speak.

She had horses who screamed out of fear of the silence, who

carried knives to protect themselves from ghosts.

She had horses who waited for destruction.

She had horses who waited for resurrection.

She had some horses.

She had horses who got down on their knees for any saviour.

She had horses who thought their high price had saved them.

She had horses who tried to save her, who climbed in her

bed at night and prayed.

She had some horses.

She had some horses she loved.

She had some horses she hated.

These were the same horses.

她的马，在黑暗中低吟，惧怕发声。
她的马，因不甘寂静而嘶鸣，
身佩利刃，为的是对付幽灵。
她的马，等待毁灭，
她的马，期待重生。
她曾有几匹马。

她的马，见到救世主就双膝跪地。
她的马，以为这高昂的代价会将他们拯救。
她的马，力图将她拯救，夜晚爬上她的床头，
祈祷。
她曾有几匹马。

她曾有几匹马，她钟爱的马。
她曾有几匹马，她憎恨的马。
这些是同一群马！

Remember

Remember the sky you were born under,

know each of the star's stories.

Remember the sun's birth at dawn, that is the

strongest point of time. Remember sundown

and the giving away to night.

Remember the moon; remember the dark.

Remember your birth, how you were given breath.

You were given laughter; you were given crying.

Remember the earth whose skin you are:

red earth, black earth, yellow earth, white earth

brown earth: we are earth.

Remember the plants, trees, animal life who all have their

tribes, their families, their histories, too. Talk to them;

listen to them. They are alive.

Remember the winds. Remember their voices. They know the

origin of this universe.

Remember you are all people and all people

are you.

Remember you are this universe and this

牢 记

牢记你出生时的那片蓝天，

熟知每一颗星星的故事。

牢记太阳诞生于黎明，那是

最为壮观的时刻。牢记落日之后，

夜晚才会登场。

牢记月亮；牢记黑暗。

牢记你诞生的一刻，你如何拥有了生命。

你会欢歌笑语；也会痛哭流涕。

牢记这片土地，你是它的肌肤：

红色的土地、黑色的土地、黄色的土地、白色的土地、

棕色的土地，我们就是整个地球。

牢记这一草一木、一花一树、一鸟一兽、一虫一物。

它们都有自己的族群，也有自己的历史。与它们畅谈吧，

聆听它们的倾诉。它们是鲜活的生命。

牢记风儿。牢记风声。它们知晓

宇宙的缘起。

牢记你是所有人，所有人

皆是你。

牢记你就是这个宇宙，

universe is you.

Remember all is in motion, is growing, is you.

Remember. Remember.

这个宇宙就是你。

牢记万物皆运动，皆成长，牢记这一切包括了你！

牢记，千万要牢记！

Anchorage
for Audre Lorde

This city is made of stone, of blood, and fish.

There are Chugatch Mountains to the east

and whale and seal to the west.

It hasn't always been this way, because glaciers

who are ice ghosts create oceans, carve earth

 and shape this city here, by the sound.

They swim backwards in time.

Once a storm of boiling earth cracked open

the streets, threw open the town.

It's quiet now, but underneath the concrete

is the cooking earth,

       and above that, air

which is another ocean, where spirits we can't see

are dancing   joking   getting full

on roasted caribou, and the praying

goes on, extends out.

锚 地
（为奥德烈·罗尔蒂[①]而作）

城市是由石头、鲜血和鱼铸就。
楚加奇山脉[②]位于城东
而鲸鱼和海豹则生活在西面。
这也并非一成不变，因为冰川是
冰之魔鬼，凭借声响，造就海洋、斧凿地球、
塑造城市。
他们在光阴岁月里游弋回溯。

曾经，翻滚的地球兴风作浪
横扫街道，摧垮城镇。
如今，风平浪静，但在混凝土下
热浪汹涌，如火如荼；
　　　　　　地表之上，是空气
造就的另一个海洋，我们无法看清
空气之灵的纵舞，　戏耍，　饕餮饱尝
烧烤后的驯鹿，祈祷
在持续，在蔓延。

---

① 美国诗人，女权主义者。
② 楚加奇山脉（Chugatch Moutains）位于阿拉斯加的中南部地区，是北美西部太平洋沿岸山脉的最北端。

Nora and I go walking down 4th Avenue
and know it is all happening.
On a park bench we see someone's Athabascan
grandmother, folded up, smelling like 200 years
of biood and piss, her eyes closed against some
unimagined darkness, where she is buried
in an ache in which nothing makes sense.

We keep on breathing, walking, but softer now,
the clouds whirling in the air above us.
What can we say that would make us understand
better than we do already?
Except to speak of her home and claim her
as our own history, and know that our dreams
don't end here, two blocks away from the ocean
where our hearts still batter away at the muddy shore.

And I think of the 6th Avenue jail, of mostly Native
and Black men, where Henry told about being shot at
eight times outside a liquor store in L.A., but when
the car sped away he was surprised he was alive,

我与诺拉沿着第四大街漫步
知晓这一切都在发生。
公园的长椅上是阿萨巴斯卡①的
老祖母，被人裹紧，臭味熏天
双眼紧闭，早已与难以想象的黑暗世界
远离。而她将会在此埋葬，
悲惨痛苦，对她来说已毫无意义。

我们生命尚存，闲庭信步，只是脚步更加轻柔，
天空飘浮朵朵白云。
是什么让我们对过往云烟
理解得如此透彻？
除却谈论她的家园，把她
当作我们曾有过的历史。我们的梦想没有
在此终结，在距离两个街区外的大海
我们的心房仍旧撞击着泥泞的海岸。

我想起了第六大街的监狱，几乎全是土著人
和黑人，在那里亨利曾诉说过在洛杉矶的一个烟酒店外，
他被八次谋杀的经历，
汽车飞速驶过后，他惊讶，自己竟然还活着，

①　阿萨巴斯卡人（Athabascan）系居住在北美洲的印第安人，主要分布在美国的阿拉斯加、加拿大和墨西哥一带。

no bullet holes, man, and eight cartridges strewn
on the sidewalk all around him.

Everyone laughed at the impossibility of it,
but also the truth. Because who would believe
the fantastic and terrible story of all of our survival
those who were never meant

to survive?

没有枪眼，天啊，八枚子弹
散落于他身旁的人行道上。

人们嘲笑这是天方夜谭，
但事实的确如此。因为有谁会相信
这传奇般的惊悚故事，九死一生，
却在那些注定不能存活

               的人身上发生？

The Woman Hanging from the Thirteenth Floor Window

She is the woman hanging from the 13th floor
window. Her hands are pressed white against the
concrete moulding of the tenement building. She
hangs from the 13th floor window in east Chicago,
with a swirl of birds over her head. They could
be a halo, or a storm of glass waiting to crush her.

She thinks she will be set free.

The woman hanging from the 13th floor window
on the east side of Chicago is not alone.
She is a woman of children, of the baby, Carlos
and of Margaret, and of Jimmy who is the oldest.
She is her mother's daughter and her father's son.
She is several pieces between the two husbands
she has had. She is all the women of the apartment
building who stand watching her, watching themselves.

When she was young she ate wild rice on scraped down
plates in warm wood rooms. It was in the farther

在十三楼窗边寻短见的女子

她就是那个在十三楼窗边寻短见的
女子。手，惨白，紧贴着
经济公寓楼的水泥装饰条。她
在芝加哥东部，十三楼的窗边寻了短见，
一群鸟儿在她的头顶盘旋。那或许是
一个光环，抑或是要将她割破的玻璃碎片。

她认为自己将获得解脱。

芝加哥东部，那个在十三楼窗边寻短见的女子
并非孤身一人。
她是孩子们的母亲，卡洛斯和玛格丽特还是婴儿，
最年长的吉米也未成年。
她是母亲的女儿、父亲的儿子。
她被两任丈夫撕成了碎片。
她是公寓楼里所有女子的代表，
她们正驻足旁观，也在深省自己。

青春年少，她在温暖的小木屋里嚼食着菰米
直到盘子上滴米不剩。那是在遥远的

north and she was the baby then. They rocked her.

She sees Lake Michigan lapping at the shores of
herself. It is a dizzy hole of water and the rich
live in tall glass houses at the edge of it. In some
places Lake Michigan speaks softly, here, it just sputters
and butts itself against the asphalt. She sees
other buildings just like hers. She sees other
women hanging from many−floored windows
counting their lives in the palms of their hands
and in the palms of their children's hands.

She is the woman hanging from the 13th floor window
on the Indian side of town. Her belly is soft from
her children's births, her worn levis swing down below
her waist, and then her feet, and then her heart.
She is dangling.

The woman hanging from the 13th floor hears voices.
They come to her in the night when the lights have gone
dim. Sometimes they are little cats mewing and scratching
at the door, sometimes they are her grandmother's voice,
and sometimes they are gigantic men of light whispering
to her to get up, to get up, to get up. That's when she wants

北方，当时，她还是个婴儿。大人们会把她左右摇晃。

她看见密歇根湖的湖水拍向了她。
那是一个令人眩晕的水洞，
周边是富人居住的玻璃房屋。在某些
地方，密歇根湖会轻声低吟，于此，湖水飞溅
拍打岸边的沥青路。她看见了
与她住所一样的建筑物。她看见了
在高层建筑的窗边轻生的其他女子。
她们的命运在自己的手中掌握
她们的命运在子女的手中掌握。

那个在十三楼窗边寻短见的女子，
居住在镇上印第安人的聚集地。孩子降生后，腹部柔软，
磨白的牛仔裤松松垮垮
及腰间，随后，双足衰老，心脏衰竭。
步履蹒跚。

那个在十三楼窗边寻短见的女子听到了声响。
夜晚，灯光昏暗，他们向她靠近。
有时，它们是喵喵叫的小猫，爪子
在抓门；有时，他们是老祖母的声音，
有时，他们是身材魁梧的男人在轻声
呼唤：起床，起床吧，起床。正当漆黑的夜晚

to have another child to hold onto in the night, to be able
to fall back into dreams.

And the woman hanging from the 13th floor window
hears other voices. Some of them scream out from below
for her to jump, they would push her over. Others cry softly
from the sidewalks, pull their children up like flowers and gather
them into their arms.
They would help her, like themselves.

But she is the woman hanging from the 13th floor window,
and she knows she is hanging by her own fingers, her
own skin, her own thread of indecision.

She thinks of Carlos, of Margaret, of Jimmy.
She thinks of her father, and of her mother
She thinks of all the women she has been, of all
the men. She thinks of the color of her skin, and
of Chicago streets, and of waterfalls and pines.
She thinks of moonlight nights, and of cool spring storms.
Her mind chatters like neon and northside bars.
She thinks of the 4 a.m. lonelinesses that have folded
her up like death, discordant, without logical and
beautiful conclusion. Her teeth break off at the edges.

她渴望将另一个孩子拥入臂弯
返回甜美的梦乡。

那个在十三楼窗边寻短见的女子听到了
其他的声响。有些人在楼下高声尖叫
因她要纵身跳下，他们会把她推下去。另一些人从
人行道上低声呼喊，像擎花朵一样把孩子们高高举起，
然后又将他们揽在怀里。
他们帮助她，如同帮自己。

然而，那依旧是在十三楼窗边寻短见的女子，
她知道把自己悬在那里，凭借的是她的手指、她的
肌肤、她细弱游丝的信念。

她挂念卡洛斯、玛格丽特和吉米。
她惦念她的父亲，还有她的母亲
她思念她所扮演的所有女子和交往的所有
男子。她顾念她的肤色，
她怀念芝加哥的小街、瀑布和松柏。
她眷恋月光的夜晚和清冷狂暴的春雨。
思想闪出碰撞的火花，如同霓虹灯与北面酒吧的灯光，交相辉映。
她想念凌晨四点的孤独
那感觉将她紧紧围裹，恰如死亡，两者如此不和，不合逻辑，
也没有美好的结局。她的牙齿边缘被磕掉。

She would speak.

The woman hangs from the 13th floor crying for
the lost beauty of her own life. She sees the
sun falling west over the grey plane of Chicago.
She thinks she remembers listening to her own life
break loose, as she falls from the 13th floor
window on the east side of Chicago, or as she
climbs back up to claim herself again.

她依然能讲话。

那个在十三楼窗边寻短见的女子哀嚎，为了
生命中失落的华彩。她看到了
日薄西山，太阳已经坠入芝加哥暗灰色的地平线。
当她从芝加哥东部的十三楼上坠落，
她内心感到了生命的流逝，或许
她可以重返人间，揭开
生命的新篇章。

From *She Had Some Horses*

I Give You Back

I release you, my beautiful and terrible
fear. I release you. You were my beloved
and hated twin, but now, I don't know you
as myself. I release you with all the
pain I would know at the death of
my children.

You are not my blood anymore.

I give you back to the soldiers
who burned down my home, beheaded my children,
raped and sodomized my brothers and sisters.
I give you back to those who stole the
food from our plates when we were starving.

I release you, fear, because you hold
these scenes in front of me and I was born
with eyes that can never close.

I release you

拱手承让

我放开你的手，我美丽而可怕的
恐惧。我放开你的手。你是我
爱恨交织的矛盾合体。如今，你我
陌路殊途。我放开你的手，
满心痛苦，如同我的孩子香消玉殒。

你已不再是我的血脉。

我把你拱手承让给了士兵
他曾焚毁我的住房，杀戮我的孩子，
强暴我的姐妹，鸡奸我的兄弟。
我把你拱手承让给了士兵
他们偷走了我们盘中的食物，我们饥肠辘辘。

我放开了你的手，恐惧，因为你在我面前
制造了这样的场面，而我生来就
有一双永远无法闭合的眼睛。

我放开了你的手。

An American Sunrise
美洲的黎明

I release you

I release you

I release you

I am not afraid to be angry.

I am not afraid to rejoice.

I am not afraid to be black.

I am not afraid to be white.

I am not afraid to be hungry.

I am not afraid to be full.

I am not afraid to be hated.

I am not afraid to be loved.

to be loved, to be loved, fear.

Oh, you have choked me, but I gave you the leash.

You have gutted me but I gave you the knife.

You have devoured me, but I laid myself across the fire.

I take myself back, fear.

You are not my shadow any longer.

I won't hold you in my hands.

You can't live in my eyes, my ears, my voice

my belly, or in my heart my heart

我放开了你的手。
我放开了你的手。
我放开了你的手。

我不再担心愤怒。
我不再担心欢愉。
我不再担心黝黑的外表。
我不再担心雪白的肌肤。
我不再担心食不果腹。
我不再担心大块朵颐。
我不再担心遭到憎恨。
我不再担心被人倾慕。

被人倾慕，被人倾慕，恐惧。

哦，你扼住了我的脖颈，我却给你递上锁链。
你对我开膛破肚，我却愿意递上屠刀。
你已将我吞噬，我却躺在火上将自己烧烤。

我找回了自我，恐惧。
你不再是我的阴影。
我不再握牢你的手。
你不会生活在我的眼中，我的耳中，我的歌中，
我的腹中，我的心中，我的心中，

my heart my heart

But come here, fear

I am alive and you are so afraid

of dying.

我的心中，我的心中。

但是，来吧，恐惧，
我还活着。而你面对死亡，
却惊慌失措。

From *Secrets From the Center of the World*

My House Is the Red Earth

My house is the red earth; it could be the center of the world.
I've heard New York, Paris, or Tokyo called the center of the
world, but I say it is magnificently humble. You could drive by
and miss it. Radio waves can obscure it. Words cannot
construct it, for there are some sounds left to sacred wordless form.
For instance, that fool crow, picking through trash near the
corral, understands the center of the world as greasy scraps of fat.
Just ask him. He doesn't have to say that the earth has turned
scarlet through fierce belief, after centuries of heartbreak and
laughter —he perches on the blue bowl of the sky, and laughs.

我的房间是红地球

我的房间是红地球，是世界的最中央。
纽约，巴黎或东京是世界中心？
的确令人汗颜！开车飞驰而过，
就可以将其甩在脑后。半导体电波也可以将它们屏蔽。
语言无法将其构建，因为有许多声响幻作了无言的神圣形式。诸
如，那个傻瓜般的乌鸦，在畜栏边的垃圾堆里寻寻觅觅，
自以为嘴里油腻腻的肥肉便是世界中心。只消
问他一句。他不必回复说，地球因为炙热的信仰，变成
了血红色，经历了百年的心碎与
狂笑——他依然在湛蓝的苍穹下栖息，大笑不已。

From *A Map to the Next World*

Emergence

It's midsummer night. The light is skinny;

a thin skirt of desire skims the earth.

Dogs bark at the musk of other dogs

and the urge to go wild.

I am lingering at the edge

of a broken heart, striking relentlessly

against the flint of hard will.

It's coming apart.

And everyone knows it.

So do squash erupting in flowers

the color of the sun.

So does the momentum of grace

gathering allies

in the partying mob.

The heart knows everything.

I remember when there was no urge

to cut the land or each other into pieces,

when we knew how to think

in beautiful.

There is no world like the one surfacing.

浮　现

仲夏的夜晚。灯光稀稀落落；
一袭欲望的薄衣掠过尘世
狗儿们追逐着另一群狗的气味
和疯狂的冲动而狂吠。
我徘徊在伤心绝望的边缘
与坚不可摧的意志
无情地搏击。
意志已经四分五裂。
所有人都已心知肚明。
它压抑了花朵的绽放
褪去了太阳的光芒。
恩泽的力量
聚在一起
却是个纵情狂欢后的暴徒。
内心洞悉一切。
我记得那个不再有冲动
去割地或是互相残杀的时代，
我还记得那个知晓以美好的情感
去思忖考量的岁月。
没有人是表里如一。

I can smell it as I pace in my square room,

the neighbor's television

entering my house by waves of sound

Makes me think about buying

a new car, another kind of cigarette

when I don't need another car

and I don't smoke cigarettes.

A human mind is small when thinking

of small things.

It is large when embracing the maker

of walking, thinking and flying.

If I can locate the sense beyond desire,

I will not cat or drink

until I stagger into the earth

with grief.

I will locate the point of dawning

and awaken

with the longest day in the world.

我在方方正正的房间里踱步，嗅到了
邻家电视里
闯进来的一阵阵声波
诱使我考虑去买
一辆新车，换个香烟的牌子
而此刻我不需要新车
也不再想吸烟。
人类渺小，当他们思虑着
微不足道的事情。
人类伟大，当他们接受了
对行走、思维与飞翔的创新。
倘若我能体会到穿越欲望的感觉，
我不会寻欢作乐，花天酒地
直到当我跌跌撞撞、痛苦地闯入地球
带着忧伤。
我会在黎明来临的那一刻
苏醒
度过世间最漫长的一日。

Songline of Dawn

We are ascending through the dawn

the sky, blushed with the fever

of attraction.

I don't want to leave my daughter,

or the babies.

I can see their house, a refuge in the dark near the university.

Protect them, oh gods of the scarlet light

who love us fiercely despite our acts of stupidity

our utter failings.

May this morning light be food for their bones,

for their spirits dressed

in manes of beautiful black hair

in skins the color of the earth as it meets the sky.

Higher we fly over the valley of monster bones

left scattered in the dirt to remind us that breathing

is rooted somewhere other than the lungs.

My spirit approaches with reverence

because it harbors the story, of how these beloveds appeared to fail

then climbed into the sky to stars of indigo.

And we keep going past the laughter and tears

黎明之梦的轨迹

我们穿过黎明，一路飞翔

碧空，披上了红霞

               魅力无限。

我不愿意离开我的女儿，

或其他小宝贝。

我能看到他们的房子，大学旁阴暗处的一个避难所。

庇护他们吧，哦，闪耀着红色之光的神灵啊

你对我们如此热爱，即便我们有愚蠢的行为

犯了彻头彻尾的错误。

愿清晨的阳光是他们骨骼的圣餐，

为他们的灵魂

披上浓密而漂亮的黑发

为他们染上天地连接处的色彩。

我们飞过山谷，越飞越高

散落在泥土里的魔鬼的尸骨提示我们，

生命会在某个地方出现，而绝不仅仅只有人类。

             我的灵魂满怀敬意地靠近

因为它内心隐藏着故事，思虑着亲爱的人们如何陨落

然后悄然飞向那靛蓝色的星空。

           我们体会了宝贝们的欢笑与泪水

of the babies who will grow up to become a light field

just beyond us.

And then the sun breaks over the yawning mountain.

And the plane shivers as we dip toward

      an old volcanic field.

It is still smoldering

motivated by the love of one deity for another.

It's an old story and we're in it so deep we have become them.

The sun leans on one elbow after making love

           savoring the wetlands just off the freeway.

We are closer to the gods than we ever thought possible.

他们终究要长大成人，充满阳光

青出于蓝而胜于蓝。

随后，阳光刺破了懒洋洋、打着哈欠的山脉。

飞机在战栗，当我们掠过

         一片古老的火山岩地。

火山岩地缓慢燃烧

是因为神祇们的爱恋。

那是个古老的故事，我们寓于其中，成了故事的主人公。

云雨之后的太阳用胳膊肘支撑

             欣赏着远离高速公路的湿地。

我们靠近神灵的距离，已经超出了我们的想象。

This Is My Heart

This is my heart. It is a good heart.
Bones and a membrane of mist and fire
are the woven cover.
When we make love in the flower world
my heart is close enough to sing
to yours in a language that has no use
for clumsy human words.

My head, is a good head, but it is a hard head
and it whirrs inside with a swarm of worries.
What is the source of this singing, it asks
and if there is a source why can't I see it
right here, right now
as real as these hands hammering
the world together
with nails and sinew?

This is my soul. It is a good soul.
It tells me, "come here forgetful one."
And we sit together with lilt of small winds

这是我的心

这是我的心，一颗善良的心。
骨骼、迷雾和火焰编织在一起，
是心的华盖。
当我们在花海里翻云覆雨
我们的心彼此贴近，我的歌声和着
你的歌声，一切人类笨拙的语言都是
那样苍白无力。

我的头脑，是聪慧的头脑，异常坚硬
它嗡嗡作响，万千惆怅。
什么是这歌声的源头，它质疑
既然有源头，为什么此时此刻，
我却看不见？
那双长有指甲和肌肉的手掌
却切切实实地
将这个世界敲击。

这是我的灵魂，一个高尚的灵魂。
它悄声告诉我："来吧，健忘的人。"
于是，我们促膝而坐，小叶栎间

who rattle the scrub oak.
We cook a little something
to eat, then a sip of something
sweet, for memory.

This is my song. It is a good song.
It walked forever the border of fire and water
climbed ribs of desire to my lips to sing to you.
Its new wings quiver with vulnerability.
Come lie next to me, says my heart.
Put your head here.
It is a good thing, says my soul.

微风徐来。
我们一起做点儿
饭吃，尝一口
甜点，
只为追忆。

这是我的歌，一首动听的歌。
它永远穿梭于水与火之间
登上欲望的肋骨，溜到我的唇边，为你歌唱。
它新生的翅膀，不堪一击。
我的心儿说道："来吧，躺在我身旁。"
"把你的头放这儿。"
"这是多么美好"，我的灵魂在低吟。

Morning Song

The red dawn now is rearranging the earth

Thought by thought

Beauty by beauty

Each sunrise a link in the ladder

Thought by thought

Beauty by beauty

The ladder the backbone

Of shimmering deity

Thought by thought

Beauty by beauty

Child stirring in the web of your mother

Do not be afraid

Old man turning to walk through the door

Do not be afraid

晨　曲

晓初大地晨曦沐浴，

万千思绪绵延千里，

�人倾国的美丽！

红日节节登上天衢，

万千思绪绵延千里，

倾人倾国的美丽！

熠熠女神冉冉升起，

万千思绪绵延千里，

倾人倾国的美丽！

小儿揽于慈母怀，

莫失措！

老人转身穿门过，

莫恐慌！

From *Conflict Resolution for Holy Beings*

This Morning I Pray for My Enemies

And whom do I call my enemy?

An enemy must be worthy of engagement.

I turn in the direction of the sun and keep walking.

It's the heart that asks the question, not my furious mind.

The heart is the smaller cousin of the sun.

It sees and knows everything.

It hears the gnashing even as it hears the blessing.

The door to the mind should only open from the heart.

An enemy who gets in, risks the danger of becoming a friend.

清晨，我为我的敌人祈祷

我把谁唤作敌人？

敌人一定要与我旗鼓相当。

我朝着太阳的方向前进，永不停歇。

问题盘旋于心底，而非被怒气冲昏的脑海。

心脏是太阳的小表弟。

它洞悉一切。

它听到了咬牙切齿的怒气，也听到了祝福。

智慧的大门只能从心底打开。

敌人闯了进来，冒着成为朋友的风险。

Once the World Was Perfect

Once the world was perfect, and we were happy in that world.

Then we took it for granted.

Discontent began a small rumble in the earthly mind.

Then Doubt pushed through with its spiked head.

And once Doubt ruptured the web,

All manner of demon thoughts

Jumped through—

We destroyed the world we had been given

For inspiration, for life—

Each stone of jealousy, each stone

Of fear, greed, envy, and hatred, put out the light.

No one was without a stone in his or her hand.

There we were,

Right back where we had started.

We were bumping into each other

In the dark.

And now we had no place to live, since we didn't know

How to live with each other.

Then one of the stumbling ones took pity on another

And shared a blanket.

世界曾经很完美

世界曾经很完美，我们欢欣雀跃地生活。

认为一切理当如此。

不满引起的小小涟漪呈现于世俗的意念中。

随后，猜忌削尖了脑袋往里挤。

一旦猜忌穿透纱帐，

魔鬼的思维

便会破门而入——

我们摧毁了上帝赐予的世界

为了灵感，为了生活——

每一块妒火中燃烧的石头，每一块

恐惧、贪婪、艳羡和憎恨的石头，压灭了世界的光芒。

每一个人手中都握有这样的石头。

从这里，

我们回到了人类的原点。

我们彼此碰撞

茫然不知。

我们不再有生存之地，因为我们不知道

如何才能相依共生。

接着，跌跌撞撞、摇摇晃晃的人们便会惺惺相惜

共享一张毛毯。

A spark of kindness made a light.

The light made an opening in the darkness.

Everyone worked together to make a ladder.

A Wind Clan person climbed out first into the next world.

Everyone carried a light to share.

善良的星星之火可以成为光束。

这光束刺破黑暗。

同心协力，众志成城。

风族①的人民率先开辟了未来世界。

每个人都手擎一盏灯将彼此照亮。

---

① 风族（Wind Clan）是英国小说《猫武士》（*Warriors*）中的四大族群之一，生活在荒原，主食为兔子。大多数风族猫都很瘦，并且跑得很快，喜欢开阔地，讨厌在树林或丛林中生活。

Spirit Walking in the Tundra

All the way to Nome, I trace the shadow of the plane as it walks
Over turquoise lakes made by the late spring break up
Of the Bering Sea.
The plane is so heavy with cargo load it vibrates our bones.
Like the pressure made by light cracking white ice.

Below I see pockets of marrow where sea birds nest.
Mothers are so protective they will dive humans.

I walk from the tarmac and am met by an old friend.
We drive to the launching place
And see walrus hunters set out toward the sea.
We swing to the summer camps where seal hangs on drying frames.
She takes me home.
I watch her son play video games on break from the university.

This is what it feels like, says her son, as we walk up tundra,
Toward a herd of musk ox, *when you spirit walk.*
There is a shaking, and then you are in mystery.

游荡在苔原的幽灵

前往诺姆①的路上，我瞥见飞机的影子掠过
晚春时分的绿松石湖
白令海峡冰消雪融。
背负着沉重不堪的货物，飞机颤抖，我们的骨头散了架。
重压似阳光在瓦解白色冰层时的力量。

俯视地面，瞅见一小片海鸟筑巢的栖息地。
大鸟护雏，潜入海底，人类不可企及。

走下停机坪，喜逢故友。
驱车赶往出海的地点
瞥见海象的捕猎者奔向大海。
我们掉头返回夏令营地，海豹在干木架上荡来荡去。
故友带我回了家。
瞧见她大学放假在家的儿子，在打电子游戏。

当我们在苔原游逛，正向一群麝牛靠近，
她的儿子说："这感觉恰如你的灵魂在游荡。
飘飘荡荡，随后陷入迷局。"

——————————
① 诺姆（Nome）是美国阿拉斯加州的西部港市。

Little purple flowers come up from the permafrost.
A newborn musk ox staggers around its mother's legs.

I smell the approach of someone with clean thoughts.
She is wearing designs like flowers, and a fur of ice.
She carries a basket and digging implements.
Her smell is sweet like blossoms coming up through the snow.
The spirit of the tundra stands with us, and we collect sunlight together,
We are refreshed by small winds.

We do not need history in books to know who we are
Or where we come from, I tell him.
Up here, we are near the opening in the Earth's head,
the place where the spirit leaves and returns.
Up here, the edge between life and death is thinner than
dried animal bladder.

(for Anuqsraaq and Qituvituaq) Nome, Alaska 2011

紫色的小花从冻土里绽放。

一头新生的小麝牛偎在母亲膝下，步履蹒跚，跌跌撞撞。

我嗅到了圣洁之人临近的气味。

她的穿戴似繁花，裹着晶莹冰雪似的衣衫。

她手挎提篮，拎着挖掘工具。

她甜甜的味道像透过冰雪而怒放的花朵。

苔原的灵魂与我们一道，收集阳光，

沐浴微风。

我们不需要教科书中的历史，来解释自己到底是谁，

或从哪里来，让我来告诉他。

于此，我们在地壳开裂的附近，

那是灵魂出没的地方。

于此，生与死的交界面已经模糊不清，比干枯的动物皮

囊更加轻薄。

（为奥斯拉卡和奇图威图赋诗一首）2011年于阿拉斯加诺姆市

The First Day without a Mother

In the hour of indigo, between sleep and wake—

A beloved teacher sits up on the funeral pyre—

He smiles at me through flames that are dancing as they eat—

I will see you again, is one of the names for blue—

A color beyond the human sky of mind—

One third up the ladder of blue is where we sit for grief—

I was abandoned by lovers, by ideas that leaped ahead of

time, and by a father looking for a vision he would never find—

Do not leave me again, I want to cry as the blue takes my teacher.

His ashes cool in my hands.

I'm too proud to let go the tears; they are still in me.

I keep looking back.

Maybe I have turned to salt. It burns blue, like the spirits who have already

started to call me home, up over the last earthy hill broken through with starts of

blue flowers that heal the wounded heart.

失去母亲的首日

夜色渐浓，半梦半醒——
一个受人爱戴的导师坐在葬礼的柴堆上——
他透过火光，冲我微笑，火苗跳跃，将他吞噬——
我会再次与你会面[1]，蓝色忧郁——
难以从心头排遣的颜色——
蓝调乐曲悠悠，我们难抑忧伤——
我被情人抛弃，被先进的理念遗弃，被
不断追逐缥缈幻想的父亲丢弃——
《不要再次离我远去》，蓝色忧郁笼罩着我的导师，我想哭泣。
他的骨灰在我手中冷却。
我孤傲冷峻，有泪不轻弹；但泪水却溢满我心田。
我回首过往。
或许我会变成一把盐。它燃烧成了蓝色，恰如幽魂
声声呼唤，回家吧，飞过最后一座开满
蓝色花朵的山丘——为我疗伤的蓝色花朵。

---

[1] 《我会再次与你会面》（*I Will See You Again*）也是英国爱尔兰歌唱组合"西域男孩"（Westlife）的第九张专辑《我们在哪里》（*Where We Are*）中的歌曲。

Chickadee sings at dawn.

I sit up in the dark drenched in longing.

I am carrying over a thousand names for blue that

I didn't have at dusk.

How will I feed and care for all of them?

March 13, 12 Glenpool, OK

拂晓，山雀唧啾。

黑暗中，我坐立难眠，苦思冥想。

涌出蓝色忧郁的同义词，成百上千，

日暮时分，我不再如此戚戚惘怅。

我怎能供养和释怀这如此忧伤？

2012年3月13日，于俄克拉荷马州格兰普尔。

In Mystic

My path is a cross of burning trees,

Lit by crows with fire in their beaks.

I ask the guardians of these lands for permission to enter.

I am a visitor to this history.

No one remembers to ask anymore, they answer.

What do I expect in this New England seaport town, near the

birthplace of democracy,

Where I am a ghost?

Even a casino can't make an Indian real.

Or should I say "native", or "savage", or "demon"?

And with what trade language,

I am trading a backwards look for jeopardy.

I agree with the ancient European maps.

There are monsters beyond imagination that troll the waters.

The Puritan's determined ships did fall off the edge of the world...

I am happy to smell the sea,

Walk the narrow winding streets of shops and restaurants, and

delight in the company of friends, trees, and small winds.

I would rather not speak with history but history came to me.

神　秘

我要穿过熊熊燃烧的树林，
被乌鸦喙里的火种点燃。
我请求卫兵准许我进入这片土地。
我成了这段历史的访客。
他们应答，没有人记得询问这段历史。
在这个新英格兰的海港小镇，与民主诞生的地方毗邻，
我是这里的鬼魂，
我怎可能有几多期许？
开设赌场也没办法将印第安人同化。
我本人到底是："土著人"，"野蛮人"，抑或"魔鬼"？
以怎样的交易语言，
让我们节节后退，换来的也是危机重重。
我赞赏古老的欧洲版图。
超乎想象的魔鬼在这片水域游荡。
清教徒们坚毅的航船从世界的边缘跌落……
我嗅到了海水的味道，心情舒畅
沿着狭窄蜿蜒的小路，逛着商店，品着美味，
与朋友、绿树、微风相伴。
我不愿意与历史对话，历史却向我走来。

It was dark before daybreak when the fire sparked. The men

leave on a hunt from the Pequot village here. The women

and children left behind are set afire; it's right here.

I do not want to know this. My gut knows the language of bloodshed.

Over six hundred are killed, to establish a home for God's

people, crowed the Puritan leaders in their Sunday sermons.

And then history was gone in a betrayal of smoke.

There is still burning though the walls are gone and we live

in a democracy erected over the burial ground.

This was given to me to speak.

Every poem is an effort at ceremony.

I asked for a way in.

(for Pam Uschuk) October 31, 2009

在火焰燃烧之前，总会有黎明前的黑暗。男人们

从佩科特人①的村庄出发去狩猎。女人

和孩子们留守点火炊饭，恰在此地。

我不想了解这些。我的直觉告诉我这血腥的历史。

六百多人被杀害，为给上帝的选民建立家园，

家里面住着清教徒的领袖们，布道，在星期天。

于是历史就随着背叛的硝烟而飘散。

隔阂已经消除，但是硝烟依然弥漫。我们尊崇的民主

竟耸立于坟丘之上。

民主让我发声，让我言语。

每一首诗都是这仪式上的尝试。

我在寻求以某种方式加入。

（为保罗·乌舒克而作）2009年10月31日

---

① 佩科特人（Pequot）是17世纪初住在美国康涅狄格州的一
支印第安人。

Suicide Watch

1.

I was on a train stopped sporadically at checkpoints.

What tribe are you, what nation, what race, what sex, what
unworthy soul?

2.

I could not sleep, because I could not wake up.

No mirror could give me back what I wanted.

3.

I was given a drug to help me sleep.

Then another drug to wake up.

Then a drug was given to me to make me happy.

They all made me sadder.

4.

Death will gamble with anyone.

There are many fools down here who believe they will win.

5.

You know, said my teacher, you can continue to wallow, or

You can stand up here with me in the sunlight and watch the battle.

自杀监视

1

乘坐火车，我偶尔会在检票口逗留。
你来自什么部落，什么民族，什么种族，什么性别，没
有价值的人啊，有何贵干？

2

我难以入眠，因为我不能觉醒。
任何明镜都难以鉴照我心。

3

我吞下一粒安眠药，催眠。
又含下另一剂药丸，清醒。
然后再服下一颗药，欢心。
而每一颗药丸都令我心碎。

4

死亡会与任何人赌博。
周遭有多少傻瓜妄信，他们会在这场赌局中获胜。

5

我的导师说，你明白，你可以继续堕落，或者
和他并肩站在阳光下，观赏战斗。

6.

I sat across from a girl whose illness wanted to jump over to me.

No! I said, but not aloud.

I would have been taken for crazy.

7.

We will always become those we have ever judged or
condemned.

8.

This is not mine. It belongs to the soldiers who raped the
young women on the Trail of Tears. It belongs to Andrew

6

我坐在一个姑娘对面，她的疾患要把我传染。

哦，不要！我说，但不敢高声。

怕人们会认为我癫疯痴狂。

7

我们终将和那些被我们审判、谴责过的人一样，遭人审
判、谴责。

8

这一切都不是我的。它属于在血泪之路①上强暴年轻妇
女的士兵。它属于安德鲁·杰克逊。

① 大批欧洲移民的涌入，使得那些开发较早而且经济比较发达的
美国东部地区人口骤增，因此可供种植的土地越来越少，大量的东部农民
无法承受猛涨的地价。1830年，时任美国总统的安德鲁·杰克逊（Andrew
Jackson）促使国会通过一项法令：《印第安人迁徙法案（The Indians Removal
Act）》。这项法令授权美国政府和东部的印第安部落谈判签定条约，
购买他们在东部的土地，把印第安人移居至密西西比河以西、洛基山山
脉以东的大平原地区，由美国政府负责移民的费用并每年向印第安人提
供食物和必要的武器。因为要远离自己祖祖辈辈生活的家园，印第安人
当然反对这些条约，但美国政府以大量贿赂部落酋长的手段，使得这些
条约得以通过。1833年第一批印第安人在美国军队的武装押送下被迫离
开了东部故土，到了印第安领地（Indian Territory）。印第安领地是从南
边和得克萨斯边界开始一直延伸到密苏里河中游的大平原南部地区，美
国政府原先保证这片地区是印第安人的永久居住地，并禁止白人移民这
里。后来这些保证都成了空头支票，这里也都成了白人定居者的地盘。
1838年最后一批佐治亚州的印第安人也在士兵的枪口和刺刀下含泪离开
家乡来到西部，他们移民所经过的路线就是美国西部开发史上著名的
"血泪之路"。这6年间一共有9万印第安人被迫移居到西部，其中有很
多人死在了"血泪之路"的途中。——译者注

Jackson. It belongs to the missionaries. It belongs to

the thieves of our language. It belongs to the Bureau of Indian

Affairs. It no longer belongs to me.

9.

I became fascinated by the dance of dragonflies over the river.

I found myself first there.

它属于传教士。它属于
盗用我们语言的窃贼。它属于
印第安人事务管理局。它已不再属于我。

9

我被小河边蜻蜓的舞步弄得神魂颠倒。
在那里，我第一次找到了自我。

Speaking Tree

"I had a beautiful dream I was dancing with a tree."

Sandra Cisneros

Some things on this earth are unspeakable:
Genealogy of the broken—
a shy wind threading leaves after a massacre,
or the smell of coffee and no one there—

Some humans say trees are not sentient beings,
but they do not understand poetry—

Nor can they hear the singing of trees when they are fed by
Rain, or bird music—
Or hear their cries of anguish when they are broken and bereft—

会说话的树

"我曾有一个美丽的梦想，我在与一棵树共舞！"
——桑德拉·希斯内罗丝[1]

有些事的确难以言说：
受害者的家谱——
一场大屠杀之后，羞涩的风穿过树叶，
咖啡的香味飘来，却不再有人品味——

常言道，草木无情，
但人们也无法埋解诗的情怀——

人们也从未听懂草木繁华滋硕之时的歌声，
也从未听懂鸟儿的欢歌笑语——
抑或是鸟儿肝肠寸断的哀鸣？

---

[1] 桑德拉·希斯内罗丝（Sandra Cisneros，1954— ），墨西哥裔美国作家，代表作有《芒果街上的小屋》（*The House on Mango Street*，1984）、短篇小说集《喊女溪及其他》（*Woman Hollering Creek and Other Stories*，1991）等。

Now I am a woman longing to be a tree, planted in a moist,
dark earth
Between sunrise and sunset—

I cannot walk through all realms—
I carry a yearning I cannot bear alone in the dark—

What shall I do with all this heartache?

The deepest–rooted dream of a tree is to walk
Even just a little ways, from the place next to the doorway—
To the edge of the river of life, and drink—

I have heard trees talking, long after the sun has gone down:

我是一个女人，渴望成为一棵树，扎根于潮湿、
黝暗泥土里的树。
昼夜轮回——

我寸步难行
我朝思暮想，我无法承载黑暗中的孤寂。

伤心欲绝，奈何？

树的梦想是成为一棵会走路的树
哪怕只是几小步，能从出生的地方踱到大门口，
踱到生命之河的边缘，吸吮甘霖——

日薄西山，我听到树在倾诉衷肠：

An American Sunrise
美洲的黎明

Imagine what would it be like to dance close together
in this land of water and knowledge...

To drink deep what is undrinkable.

"展开想象的翅膀，我们一起欢歌曼舞
在水份充足、充满智慧的大地上……"

"吸吮那难以企及的滋养。"

Sunrise

Sunrise, as you enter the houses of everyone here, find us.

We've been crashing for days, or has it been years.

Find us, beneath the shadow of this yearning mountain, crying here.

We have been sick with sour longings, and the jangling of fears.

Our spirits rise up in the dark, because they hear,

Doves in cottonwoods calling forth the sun.

We struggled with a monster and lost.

Our bodies were tossed in the pile of kill. We rotted there.

We were ashamed and we told ourselves for a thousand years,

We didn't deserve anything but this—

And one day, in relentless eternity, our spirits discerned movement of prayers

Carried toward the sun.

And this morning we are able to stand with all the rest

And welcome you here.

We move with the lightness of being, and we will go

Where there's a place for us.

日　出

日出东方，你闯进了每个人的房间，寻到了我们。

我们已争吵数日，抑或是累月经年。

渴望沐浴阳光的山峦，在它的阴影下，你会察觉，我们在哭泣。

我们已经厌倦了那痛苦的憧憬和令人局促不安的恐惧。

我们的灵魂在幽暗中升起，因为听到了，

棉白杨树上的鸽子呼唤阳光。

我们与魔鬼抗争，最终以失败收场。

我们的尸体被抛起，百般摧残。我们在那里溃烂。

我们羞愧不已，我们自言自语上千年，

我们不值一文，但是——

终有一天，不屈不挠，我们的灵魂会目睹

递给太阳的祷文。

这个清晨，我与伙伴们一起

迎接你的到来。

我们跟随生命的光影移动，我们将要奔赴

那个属于我们的地方。

Do Not Feed the Monster

Do not feed the monsters.

Some are wandering thought forms, looking for a place to set up house.

Some are sent to you deliberately. They can come from

arrows or gossip, jealousy or envy.

Or inadvertently from just...thoughtlessness.

Instead, have a party.

Invite your helpers to the table. Give them something to do.

They want to be helpful.

Celebrate.

Feed the birds.

不要给魔鬼投食

不要给魔鬼投食。

有些魔鬼正徘徊于你思绪的洪流，寻觅安家的落脚点。

有些魔鬼处心积虑地闯入你的领地。他们可能来自

弓箭或是谣言，猜忌或是艳羡。

他们也可能是漫不经心⋯⋯心不在焉。

管它呢，开个晚会吧，

盛邀帮助过你的朋友。请他们做点事儿吧。

他们乐于助人。

庆贺吧！

只把美食投给鸟儿。

Conflict Resolution for Holy Being

"I am the holy being of my mother's prayer and my father's song. "
—Norman Patrick Brown, Dineh poet and speaker

1. Set conflict resolution ground rules:

Whose lands are these on which I stand,

I ask the deer, turtle, and the crane?

Have I asked the right questions?

Have the spirits of these lands been respected and treated with good will?

Or are they soaked in blood of ingratitude?

The land remembers everything.

The red shimmer of remembering compels us up the night to

walk to our children's rooms to check on their safety, their

innocence, and their right to call a path of joy.

This morning as I brushed my hair over the hotel sink to get ready I heard:

We must listen and by listening we will understand our

names, and the names by which our grandchildren shall speak—

为圣人消解冲突

"我是母亲祷文和父亲圣歌里的圣人。"
——诺曼·帕特里克·布朗，纳瓦霍①诗人与演说家

1. 消解冲突的基本原则

我脚下的土地是谁的？
我向小鹿、海龟和仙鹤询问。
我问的问题没错吧？
这土地的灵魂是否被厚爱和善意地款待？
还是被浸泡在忘恩负义的血水里？
土地会牢记这一切。
记忆的亮光驱使我们在深夜
踏进孩子们的卧房以确保他们平平安安、
天真无邪，并享有快乐的权利。
清晨，我梳理头发，在旅馆的洗脸池边，预备好倾听：
也务必要聆听，由此，我们才会理解我们的
名字，我们将会被子子孙孙呼唤的名字——

---

① 美国最大的印第安人部落是纳瓦霍人（Navojo）。Dineh
是纳瓦霍人对自己本种族的称呼。

We do not parade, pleased with ourselves.

We must speak in the language of justice.

2. Use effective communication skills that display and enhance mutual trust and respect:

If you sign this paper we will become brothers. We will no longer fight. We will give you this land and these waters "as long as the grass shall grow and the rivers run".

The lands and waters they gave us did not belong to them to give. Under false pretenses we signed. After drugging by drink, we signed. With a mass of gun power pointed at us, we signed. With a flotilla of war ships at our shores, we signed. We are still signing. We have found no peace in this act of signing.

A casino was raised up over the gravesite of our ancestors. Our own distant cousins pulled up the bones of grandparents, parents and grandchildren from their last sleeping place. They had forgotten how to be human beings. Restless winds emerged from the earth when the graves were open and the winds went looking for justice.

我们不再炫耀，自得其乐。
我们必须以正义的语言道出心声。

2. 用有效的交流手段来展示和加强双方的信任与尊重

如果你签署了这份文件，我们就成了兄弟。我们将不再争斗。我们会把这片土地和水域交付于你，"只要你保证青草能够生长，河水还会流淌"。

他们赠与我们的土地和水域并不属于他们自己，也无权赠与。 在骗局的引诱下，我们签署了文件。在欢饮迷醉之后，我们签署了文件。在枪口的威逼下，我们签署了文件。在战船驶进我们海岸的一刻，我们签署了文件。我们一直在不断地签署文件，却无法因为文件的签署而获得和平。

我们祖先的墓地上盖起了赌场。我们远房的堂兄妹们将祖辈、父辈还有孙辈的尸骨从他们最后长眠的地方掘起。他们已经忘却了自己曾是人类。坟墓被撬开的一刻，
风不停地从地面刮起，
风也在不断地寻觅公平正义。

If you raise this white flag of peace, we will honor it.

At Sand Creek several hundred women, children and men were slaughtered in an unspeakable massacre, after a white flag was raised. The American soldiers trampled the white flag in the blood of the peacemakers.

There is a suicide epidemic among native children. It is triple the rate of the rest of America. "It feels like wartime," said a child welfare worker in South Dakota.

If you send your children to our schools we will train them to get along in this changing world. We will educate them.

如果你升起和平的白旗，我们会向它致意。

沙溪河畔，白旗已被举起，几百个妇女、儿童和男人却被不可理喻地杀戮。美国大兵践踏了这白旗，沾满了和平缔造者的鲜血。[1]

自杀的倾向在印第安儿童当中不断蔓延。这里的自杀率是美国其他地方的三倍。"那感觉就像是处于战争年代"，一名在南达科他州的儿童福利工作者说道。

如果你们将孩子送到我们的学校，我们对他们进行培训，让他们适应这个变化多端的世界。我们会让他们受教育。

---

[1] 这里指的是沙溪大屠杀（Sand Creek Massacre），又称奇温顿大屠杀（Chivington Massacre）或沙溪战役（Battle of Sand Creek），即夏安族印第安人屠杀事件（Massacre of Cheyenne Indians）。这是在北美印第安战争期间发生的一起战争犯罪事件。1864年11月29日，约700名隶属于科罗拉多州第三骑兵军团的士兵，无预警地袭击了居住在科罗拉多州南方印第安保留地的一个印第安人部落，当地居住着约200余名夏安族及阿拉巴霍族（Arapaho）居民。这些居民遭到了军队无情的屠杀，估计造成了70名至163名印第安人的死亡，其中2/3是妇女及儿童。许多印第安人在死亡后遭到肢解，其头皮及身体的很多器官被美军士兵当成战利品，做成饰品。

We had no choice. They took our children. Some ran away and froze to death. If they were found they were dragged back to the school and punished. They cut their hair, took away their language, until they became as strangers to themselves even as they became strangers to us.

If you sign this paper we will become brothers. We will no longer fight. We will give you this land and these waters in exchange "as long as the grass shall grow and the rivers run".

Put your hand on this bible, this blade, this pen, this oil derrick, this gun and you will gain trust and respect with us. Now we can speak together as one.

We say, put down your papers, your tools of coercion, your promises, your lies, your posture of superiority and sit with us before the fire. We will share food, songs and stories. We will gather beneath starlight and dance, and rise together at sunrise, called to speak truth and walk a path of compassion.

The sun rose over the Potomac this morning, over the city surrounding the white house. It blazed scarlet, a fire opening

我们别无选择。他们掳走了我们的孩子。一些孩子虽逃出了魔爪，却依然被冻死。即使他们被发现时，还活着，也会被重新拽回学校，遭受惩罚。他们剪掉孩子们的头发，掠夺掉他们的语言，直到孩子们辨不清自己到底是谁，甚至我们也觉得他们如此陌生！

如果你签署了这份文件，我们就成了兄弟。我们将不再争斗。我们会拿这片土地和水域与你交换，"只要你保证青草能够生长，河水还会流淌"。

将你的手放在宝典上、刀锋上、钢笔上、钻油塔上、枪杆上，你便会赢得我们的信任与尊重。如今，我们可以一起促膝长谈，团结如一人。

我们说，放下你的文件吧，你的高压政策、你的诺言、你的谎话、你傲慢的姿态！坐下来吧，与我们偎依在炉火边。我们分享美食，引吭高歌，倾诉衷肠。我们聚集在星空下，翩翩起舞，太阳升起便起床，大胆陈述真理，踏步走上洒满同情的小路。

清晨，太阳在波拖马可河①上冉冉升起，照耀着那个白色房子周围的城市。它是耀眼的红色，象征真理的火

---

① 波拖马可河（Potomac）是美国东部重要河流，流经首都华盛顿。

truth. White House, Chogo Hvtke means the house of the
peacekeeper, the keepers of justice. We have crossed this
river to speak to the white leader for peace since these
settlers arrived in our territory and made this their place of
governance. These streets are our old trails, curved to fit
around trees.

3. Give constructive feedback:

We speak together with this trade language of English. This
trade language enables us to speak across many language
boundaries. These languages have given us the poets:

Ortiz, Silko, Momaday, Alexie, Diaz, Bird, Woody, Kane,
Bitsui, Long Soldier, White, Erdrich, Tapahonso, Howe,
Louis, Brings Plenty, Okpik, Hill, Wood, Maracle, Sewell,
Trask, Hogan, Dunn, Welch...

The 1957 Chevy is unbeatable in style. My broken down
one–eyed Ford will have to do. It holds everyone: Grandma and
grandpa, aunties and uncles, the children and the babies, and all
my boyfriends. That's what she said, anyway, as she drove off

焰。白宫，土著语唤作Chogo Hvtke，意指和平卫士的
房屋、正义战士的房屋，我们跨过这条河，与白人首领
商讨和平，自从这些殖民者踏上我们的领土，并成为这
片土地的主宰。这些街道是我们的小径、蜿蜒的林间
小路。

3. 给出富有建设性的反馈

我们用英语一起商谈，那是一种交易语言。这种交易语
言能让我们跨越诸多语言的界限。这些语言为我们造就
了很多诗人：

奥提兹, 西尔科, 莫玛蒂, 勒克斯, 迪亚斯, 伯德, 伍迪, 凯恩,
碧苏, 朗·索蒂尔, 怀特, 厄德里奇, 塔帕宏索, 豪,
路易斯, 布林斯·布兰绨, 奥皮克, 希尔,伍德, 梅拉克, 休厄尔,
特拉斯克, 霍根, 邓恩, 韦尔奇……

1957年款的雪佛兰无与伦比。我那破旧不堪、独眼龙般
的福特却在此时必须担当重任。车子装下了所有的人：
爷爷奶奶、叔叔阿姨、大大小小的孩子，还有我的历任
男友。如她自己所言，无论如何，这部一步三晃的老爷

for the Forty−Nine with all of us in that shimmying wreck.

Some of us still know how to fly to the moon.

There would be no blues, jazz—it would be different
without the circle around the fire, green corn, the joking, the
all night dancing and singing.

Get down. Get down Adolfe Sax for inventing the
saxophone. You have given us Jim Pepper, Tom Berryhill,
John Coltrane, Lester Young, Ben Webster, Joshua Redman,
Sheryl Cassity, Randy Plummer... Mvto. Thank you. Get
funky.

You might try dancing theory with a bustle, or a jingle dress,
or turtles strapped around your legs. You might try wearing

车都可以带上我们所有的人去跳四十九步舞[①]。

我们当中仍然有人知晓如何能飞往月球。

不再有蓝调和爵士乐——也不再围着篝火和绿色的玉米而整夜地说说笑笑,翩翩起舞,尽情歌唱,周遭一切将截然不同。

下车吧。下了车,阿道夫·萨克斯[②]发明了萨克斯管。你已经为我们造就了吉姆·佩琦,汤姆·贝里希尔,约翰·科尔特兰,李斯特·扬,本·韦伯斯特,乔舒亚·雷德曼,谢乐尔·卡西蒂,兰迪·普拉默……摩图。心存感激!朴实无华的爵士风。

你或许在尝试学习舞蹈理论,身着有腰垫或是铃铛的连衣裙,或者用带子将海龟绑在你的腿周围。你的穿衣打扮

---

①　四十九步舞（the Forty-Nine）是北美土著人民经常跳的一种舞蹈。过去,人们会选择在距离城市较远的地方又唱又跳,通宵达旦。现如今,人们也有可能在宾馆的房间里载歌载舞。

②　阿道夫·萨克斯(Adolfe Sax, 1814–1894),出生于比利时的迪南（Dinant）。他在1840年根据波姆式长笛的原理发明了萨克斯管,并以自己的名字命名该乐器。1846年,他又取得萨克斯管的发明专利,并于法国巴黎开办了乐器厂,专门生产萨克斯管。并先后生产了十四种萨克斯管,包括高音、小高音、中音、次中音、低音、倍低音等。

colonization like a heavy gold chain around a pimp's neck.

4. Reduce defensiveness and break the defensiveness chain:

I could hear the light beings as they entered every cell.
Every cell is a house of the god of light they said. I could
hear the spirits who love us stomp dancing. They were
dancing as if they were here, and then another level of here,
and then another, until the whole earth and sky was dancing.

We are here dancing, they said. There was no there.

There was no "I" or "you".

There was us; there was "we".

There we were as if we were the music.

You cannot legislate music to lock step nor can you legislate
the spirit of the music to stop at political boundaries—

—Or poetry, or art, or anything that is of value or matters in
this world, and the next worlds.

或许已经殖民化，比方说像皮条客那样脖颈上绕上一条沉重的金链子。

4. 减少抵触情绪，打破防御的链条

我能够听到光的小精灵闯入细胞里的声响。每一个细胞都是光明之神的居所，他们说。我能够听到深爱我们的精灵在跳顿足爵士舞。他们狂舞，恰如在我们身旁。气氛不断蔓延，再蔓延，直至整个地球和天空都狂舞起来。

我们在这里跳舞，他们说。已经没有所谓的那个地方。

"我"和"你"已经不分彼此。

只有我们；只有"我们"团结在一起。

在那个地方，我们，好像我们就是乐曲。

你没有办法为音乐制定法律来锁住你的舞步，你也不能为音乐的灵魂制定法律而让它止于政治的边缘——

——或止于诗歌、艺术，抑或是今生今世和来生来世重要而有价值的万物。

This is about getting to know each other.

We will wind up back at the blues standing on the edge of the flatted fifth about to jump into a fierce understanding together.

5. Eliminate negative attitudes during conflict:

A panther poised in the cypress tree about to jump is a panther poised in a cypress tree about to jump.

The panther is a poem of green eyes of fire, and a lean, black muscle of four circling winds.

The panther hears everything: the uncried tears of a few hundred human years, the winds that will break what has broken his world, a bluebird swaying on a branch a few miles away.

Most of all he hears the blood running of his approaching prey. The running deer follows his death song. The song is a black panther with green eyes of fire, perched in the poetry of the cypress tree.

这一切将让我们彼此相识。

我们重新跳起蓝调，停留在平缓的第五音程，为的是知此知彼，肝胆相照。

5. 于冲突中消除负面情绪

一只美洲豹栖息在松柏上，欲纵身飞跃，那是一只栖息在松柏之上的美洲豹，欲纵身一跃。

美洲豹就是一首诗，绿莹莹的目光，颀长黝黑的肌肉，生风的四爪。

美洲豹洞悉一切：那承载人类几百年历史的无声泪水，摧毁了曾破坏它家园的魔鬼的狂风，还有几英里外，摇曳在树枝上的蓝色知更鸟。

它听到最多的是猎物靠近时鲜血流淌的声音。
死亡之歌的背后是奔跑的梅花鹿。这首歌是黑色的美洲豹，带着绿莹莹的目光，栖息在松柏一样的诗行上。

6. And, use what you learn to resolve your own conflicts and to mediate others conflicts:

When we made it back home, back over those curved roads that wind through the city of peace, we stopped at the doorway of sunset as it opened to our homelands.
We gave thanks for the story, for all parts of the story because it was by the light of those challenges we learned to know ourselves—
We asked for forgiveness. We laid down our burdens next to each other.

Joy Harjo March 24, 2014 Arlington, VA

6. 用理性调停与他人的龃龉，斡旋与他人的冲突

当我们带着它返回家园，返回至弯弯曲曲的小路，一直
蜿蜒至和平之城；我们在落日余晖的家门口逗留，是它
洒满了我们的故土。
因为这样的经历，我们感恩。人生经历带给我们挑战，
由此，我们学会了认识自己——

我们祈求原谅。我们卸下千斤重担，薪火相传。

风欢乐 2014年3月24日于弗吉尼亚州的阿灵顿

New Poem

An American Sunrise

We were running out of breath, as we ran out to meet ourselves. We
Were surfacing the edge of our ancestors' fights, and ready to Strike
It was difficult to lose days in the Indian bar if you were Straight.

Easy if you played pool and drank to remember to forget. We
Made plans to be professional— and did. And some of us could Sing
So we drummed a fire lit pathway up to those starry stars. Sin

Was invented by the Christians, as was the Devil, we sang. We
Were the heathens, but needed to be saved from them: Thin
Chance. We knew we were all related in this story, a little Gin

Will clarify the dark, and make us all feel like dancing. We
Had something to do with the origins of blues and Jazz
I argued with a Pueblo as I filled the jukebox with dimes in June,

Forty years later and we still want justice. We are still America. We
Know the rumors of our demise. We spit them out. They Die Soon.

美洲的黎明

我们气喘吁吁，跑出去与自己会面，我们
正在披露祖先们好斗的特性，时刻准备好罢工
很难在印第安人的小酒吧里把岁月蹉跎，如果你够坦白、直率。

打打台球或是一醉方休，光阴虚度轻而易举。我们
制订了专业计划，我们的确如此。我们当中有人会引吭高歌
我们点燃篝火，照亮小路，星空浩瀚。原罪

是基督信徒们的创造，魔鬼也是基督信徒的手笔，我们吟唱。我们
是异教徒，并不渴望被他们拯救：微乎其微
的可能。我们知晓，在这个故事里我们彼此相连，一点点杜松子酒

便会驱散黑暗，令我们起舞翩翩。我们
与布鲁斯渊源盘根纠错，当然也包含爵士乐
我与普韦布洛①的印第安人唇枪舌剑，当我向点唱机里慷慨投币，在六月，

光阴流转四十载，我们依然需要正义。我们仍隶属美洲。我们
清楚有关我们消亡的流言蜚语。我们对此鄙视、唾弃。它们会迅速烟消云散。

---

① 普韦布洛（Pueblo）是美国科罗拉多州中部的一座城市。

Joy Harjo

——A Carrier of Memory [1]

The poet Joy Harjo acts as a guide in taking us on a journey into her identity as a woman and as an artist, poised between poetry and music, encompassing tribal heritage and productive reassessments and comparisons with the American cultural patrimony. She proudly underlines her Indian roots, and this all-embracing assertion unceasingly leaves a profoundly coherent mark on form and content.

Her success as a poet, after a relatively short period of writing, is displayed in numerous volumes. Her work is attracting a growing readership, and has drawn the attention of critics in the USA and elsewhere, as well as in several university courses dedicated to her production, giving rise to high quality degree dissertations.

She is always animated by the desire to find an area of light, sometimes in a harsh clash with reality. The first thing

---

[1] Excerpted from Laura Coltelli's introduction in *Soul Talk, Song Language, Conversations with Joy Harjo*, Wesleyan University Press, 2011.

风欢乐

——记忆的活化石 [1]

诗人风欢乐（Joy Harjo），如同一个向导，带领我们游历于她作为女性和艺术家的人生旅程，她时常逗留于诗歌与音乐之间，包容印第安部族的优秀传统，重新估量和比较美洲文化遗产。她为自己的祖先是印第安人而倍感自豪，这种兼收并蓄的主张对她诗歌的内容与形式均产生了持久而深刻的影响。

在经过了短暂的写作生涯之后，她在诗歌创作领域便大获成功，这可以从其大量的诗歌作品中略见一斑。她的作品越来越吸引读者的眼球，也越来越受美国和世界其他国家评论家的关注。同时，一些大学也开设了涉及风欢乐诗歌的课程，这导致以其诗歌为研究对象的高质量学位论文层出不穷。

她的创作总是被寻觅光明的渴望所驱使，而这种渴望有时候会与现实产生激烈的碰撞。她从事写作后所尝

---

① 节选自卫斯廉大学出版社2011年出版的《灵魂对话，歌曲的语言：与风欢乐一席谈》一书中劳拉·科尔泰利关于风欢乐的介绍。

to emerge from her writer's laboratory is the close anchoring of her poetry to orality, with the result that"written text is, for me, fixed orality": it thus goes back to a performance she remembers and it transmits an oral act, in which the moment of speaking and listening unites the poet and her audience in a single inseparable unit. Since poetry is a sound art, as she affirms, music, singing voice and spoken poetic word converge together "as one voice".

Thus Harjo's work now includes different aspects from those that it displayed initially: the written word also becomes a voice modulated with traditional tones— songs and chants, which radiate a music that springs from her saxophone. But the sonorities that come into being are not an accompaniment or a musical tempo, but rather intimate unions of words, voices and sounds which convey the blend and interpenetration of meanings and rhythms, perfectly harmonized in a continual reciprocal reflection. A performance like this goes beyond its own communicative act, and becomes the expression of a culture, as she says, captured in its deepest roots, and modulated with a sense of belonging and continuity. The contribution of modern sonorities such as blues is suggestive not so much of influences, but of a revitalization of a kind of music born and cultivated in the tribal environment. This is the

试的第一件事情就是将她的诗歌呈现出强烈的口语化色彩——"写作文本，对我来说，就是固定的口语形态"。由此，可以追溯到风欢乐记忆中的每一个言语行为，并将这个行为转化成一种口述传统，当故事陈述伴随着倾听，那一刻，诗人和听众也结合成了一个不可分割的整体。风欢乐强调说，因为诗歌是完整的艺术，音乐、歌声和口口相传的富有诗意的语言最终应该汇聚成"一个完整的声音"。

迄今，风欢乐的作品包含了很多方面，而最初展现的诗歌风格是其笔端的文字亦唤作歌声，并随着传统歌曲和圣歌的基调而转换，同时散发着她萨克斯管乐曲的气息。但是这种响亮的声音却并非音乐伴奏或节拍，而是文字、声音和音调的亲密结合，表达出意义与节奏的融合与诠释，以及二者之间始终互为依托的和谐。正如风欢乐所言，这样的言语已经远远超过了其本身的交流作用，而成为扎根于言语却又伴随归属感和延续性而转换的一种文化表达。诸如蓝调音乐这样既现代又深沉、响亮的音调未必会产生太多的影响力，但它却是一种产

awareness that animates the poetics and musical activity of Joy Harjo, intent as she is on not leaving any empty spaces between words, voice and music.

It is a language at the basis of so–called "minority literature" –Indian, in this case–a label that Harjo identifies as a "power trick", because, she affirms, the geographic expanse of tribal cultures covers an immense extension from one end of the globe to the other, including major literary traditions: "It's the fearful ones who try and keep us out who are still looking for a place." And she goes on: "This 'American culture' is young and rootless. It is adolescent with an adolescent sense of time and place, that is: 'here and now', with no reference or power rooted in the earth, ancestors or historical and mythical sense. Value your community and what that has to offer, and continue to reach out beyond what you know, and grow fresh ideas, meetings between borders, new roots."

The representation of Harjo's activity extends to the role and the responsibility of the artist: he/she must be the one who brings a testimony of experience in the present, but also a renewal in the wake of tradition; he/she promotes and regenerates art and culture, sometimes communicating with his/her public almost beyond the realm of words, if the communicative act takes place in perfect reciprocal integrity, if words are used to usher in transformation.

生和孕育于部落生存环境的、充满生命活力的音乐。这种理念促成风欢乐将诗歌和音乐结合，使得她在创作之时不会在文字、声音和音乐之间留下任何间隙。

印第安语是一种少数民族文学语言，风欢乐却把它当作一种"有力的手段"，因为，她断言，印第安民族在文化、地理上的扩展一定会从地球的这一端蔓延至另一端，甚至会影响主流文学传统。"只有那些试图将我们排斥在外的人才会感到恐惧，也只有他们才会不断地寻觅空间。"她继续坦言，"这种所谓的'美国文化'是稚嫩和无根的。它还处于青少年阶段，只具有不成熟的时间和空间概念，即'此时此地'没有任何考据和根基，没有祖先或历史和神话体系。珍惜你所处的族群和族群带给你的一切。然后，不断超越你的心智，孕育新颖的思想，在不同的国度际会，新的根基便会形成。"

风欢乐灵动思维的体现进一步反映了作为艺术家所应该承担的责任：他或她务必具备对眼前的经历进行核实、检验的能力，同时，尊重传统，并有所创新；他或她应该弘扬艺术和文化，革新艺术和文化，间或与民众进行交流，如果这种交流能够在完美的互惠互利的原则下发生，如果语言文字被用来引领变革，这种交流几乎可超越文字。

In this context, then, to write poetry "is to move into the world and effect change", and that includes the artist and his/her public, both part of the poem.

Harjo's thoughts turn instead to global roots and ancient trades by which almost everything traveled all over the world, connecting peoples and cultures. The same can be said for our creation of our own stories, which means that we pass on family, clan and tribal knowledge from one generation to another, making time and space larger than we can imagine.

But being a poet is a challenge that expands, in order to reconstruct this land called America. With the strength of writing, of poetry, of myths, it is possible to lay the foundations for the imposition of a change, and to penetrate with language into a spiral of cognitive experience, the essence that genuinely gives meaning to the life of our intellect and our spirit.

Joy Harjo lives in many different worlds. She draws a moving geography of the soul. She is always intensely dedicated to reaching, or recovering, intangible perfections or visions in her search as a woman and an artist.

在这样的背景下，诗歌创作就是"走向世界和变革的过程"，这一过程包含艺术家和民众的参与，二者也是诗歌的一部分。

风欢乐的思维也开始放眼全球，并关注古代贸易，通过这些贸易，几乎所有的东西都可以周游世界，从而将民族和文化连在一起。同理，可以说我们在创造我们自己的故事，这意味着将家庭、宗族和部落的智慧从一代人传到另一代人手中，使得时间和空间概念比我们所想象的要广阔得多。

选择"诗人"这个职业是人生的一种挑战，因为她肩负着重建这片被称作"美洲"的土地的职责。随着文字作品、诗歌和神话影响力的增强，诗人很有可能为不得不做出的变革而奠定基础，利用语言的力量穿透螺旋式上升的认知经验，从本质上说，就是确确实实为我们的思维能力和精神赋予了意义。

风欢乐生活在许多不同的"世界"。她刻画了灵魂的心路。作为女性和艺术家，她不断敦促自己达到难以企及的完美巅峰，觅回难以企及的人间美景。

风欢乐作品列表

1. *What Moon Drove Me to This?* (Poetry)

《什么样的月亮让我变成了这样》（诗集）

2. *She Had Some Horses* (Poetry)

《她曾有几匹马》（诗集）

3. *Secrets from the Center of the World* (Poetry)

《来自世界中心的秘密》（诗集）

4. *In Mad Love and War* (Poetry)

《在疯狂的爱与战争之间》（诗集）

5. *The Woman Who Fell From the Sky* (Poetry)

《从天际坠落的女子》（诗集）

6. *A Map to the Next World* (Poetry)

《一张通往来世的地图》（诗集）

7. *How We Became Human, New and Selected Poems 1975—2001* (Poetry)

《辗转成人及新诗选（1975—2001）》（诗集）

8. *Conflict Resolution for Holy Beings* (Poetry)

《为圣人消解冲突》（诗集）

9. *Soul Talk, Song Language: Conversations with Joy Harjo* （Non-fiction）

《灵魂对话，歌曲的语言：与风欢乐一席谈》（非小说）

10. *Crazy Brave: A Memoir* (Non-fiction)

《疯狂的勇敢：回忆录》（非小说）

11. *The Good Luck Cat* (Children's literature)

《幸运的猫咪》（儿童文学）

12. *For a Girl Becoming* (Children's literature)

《家有小女初长成》（儿童文学）